# The 12 Houses of Astrology and Birth Charts

*Unlock the Secrets of Natal Chart Interpretation, the Zodiac Signs, and Life's Cosmic Lessons*

© Copyright 2025 - All rights reserved.

The content contained within this book may not be reproduced, duplicated, or transmitted without direct written permission from the author or the publisher.

Under no circumstances will any blame or legal responsibility be held against the publisher, or author, for any damages, reparation, or monetary loss due to the information contained within this book, either directly or indirectly.

**Legal Notice:**

This book is copyright protected. It is only for personal use. You cannot amend, distribute, sell, use, quote or paraphrase any part, or the content within this book, without the consent of the author or publisher.

**Disclaimer Notice:**

Please note the information contained within this document is for educational and entertainment purposes only. All effort has been executed to present accurate, up-to-date, reliable, and complete information. No warranties of any kind are declared or implied. Readers acknowledge that the author is not engaging in the rendering of legal, financial, medical, or professional advice. The content within this book has been derived from various sources. Please consult a licensed professional before attempting any techniques outlined in this book.

By reading this document, the reader agrees that under no circumstances is the author responsible for any losses, direct or indirect, that are incurred as a result of the use of the information contained within this document, including, but not limited to, errors, omissions, or inaccuracies.

# Your Free Gift
# (only available for a limited time)

Thanks for getting this book! If you want to learn more about various spirituality topics, then join Mari Silva's community and get a free guided meditation MP3 for awakening your third eye. This guided meditation mp3 is designed to open and strengthen ones third eye so you can experience a higher state of consciousness. Simply visit the link below the image to get started.

https://spiritualityspot.com/meditation

Or, Scan the QR code!

# Table of Contents

**PART 1: THE TWELVE HOUSES OF ASTROLOGY** .......... 1
   INTRODUCTION .......... 3
   CHAPTER 1: ASTROLOGY BASICS .......... 5
   CHAPTER 2: MEET THE ASTROLOGICAL PLANETS .......... 14
   CHAPTER 3: NODES AND ASTEROIDS MATTER, TOO .......... 28
   CHAPTER 4: THE 12 ZODIAC SIGNS .......... 40
   CHAPTER 5: SUN, MOON, AND RISING SIGNS .......... 55
   CHAPTER 6: THE HOUSES I. EGO, RESOURCES, AND THE MIND .......... 67
   CHAPTER 7: THE HOUSES II. HOME, CREATIVITY, AND HEALTH .......... 75
   CHAPTER 8: THE HOUSES III. RELATIONSHIPS, GROWTH, AND TRAVEL .......... 82
   CHAPTER 9: THE HOUSES IV. CAREER, FRIENDSHIP, AND SPIRITUALITY .......... 89
   CHAPTER 10: PUTTING IT ALL TOGETHER: YOUR BIRTH CHART .......... 97
   EXTRA: ASTROLOGICAL SYMBOLS AND GLYPHS .......... 103
   CONCLUSION .......... 106
**PART 2: BIRTH CHARTS** .......... 109
   INTRODUCTION .......... 111
   CHAPTER 1: WHAT ARE BIRTH CHARTS? .......... 113
   CHAPTER 2: THE ASTROLOGICAL HOUSES I .......... 121
   CHAPTER 3: THE ASTROLOGICAL HOUSES II .......... 133

CHAPTER 4: MEET THE ZODIAC SIGNS ..................................................... 144
CHAPTER 5: THE ANCHORS AND ANGLES OF YOUR BIRTH CHART ........................................................................................................ 156
CHAPTER 6: PLANETS, NODES, AND ASTEROIDS ................................. 164
CHAPTER 7: MAJOR PLANETARY ASPECTS ............................................ 176
CHAPTER 8: MINOR PLANETARY ASPECTS ............................................ 184
CHAPTER 9: TYPES OF CHART ANALYSIS .............................................. 192
CHAPTER 10: HOW TO READ ANY CHART ............................................. 200
GLOSSARY OF GLYPHS ................................................................................ 211
BONUS: BIRTH CHART TEMPLATES ........................................................ 217
CONCLUSION .................................................................................................. 219
HERE'S ANOTHER BOOK BY MARI SILVA THAT YOU MIGHT LIKE ................................................................................................................... 222
YOUR FREE GIFT (ONLY AVAILABLE FOR A LIMITED TIME) ................. 223
REFERENCES ................................................................................................... 224
IMAGE SOURCES ............................................................................................ 229

# Part 1: The Twelve Houses of Astrology

*The Ultimate Guide to Themes, Lessons, Birth Chart Interpretation, and the 12 Zodiac Signs*

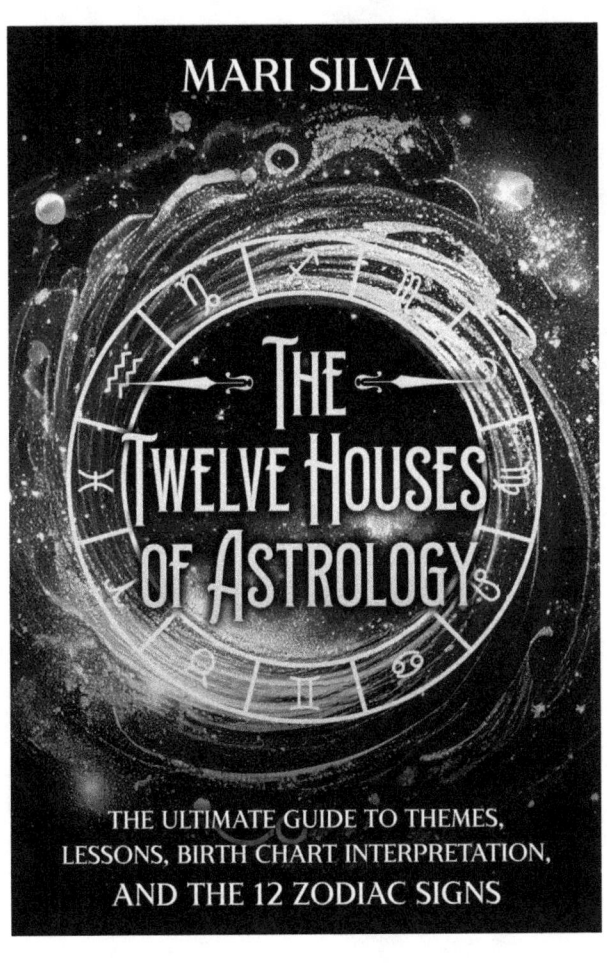

# Introduction

Have you ever wondered what makes you uniquely "you"? Astrology can provide some of the answers to that. It's an ancient science-based system that uses the individual positions of the planets, stars, and other celestial bodies to interpret the personality and potential of people.

Astrology is an ancient practice used to predict the future and gain insight into your life and personality. Many don't realize that by looking at the position of planets, stars, and other objects in space, astrology can help us better understand astronomical concepts. It forces you to engage with your world and its patterns in a whole new way, immersing you in the mysteries of the universe.

While you may not always like what this ancient art reveals about your innermost self, learning it can give you access to unique knowledge about where each planet lies as well as how all celestial bodies interact. If you're looking for a way to dive deep and get to know yourself better, astrology may be just the tool for you. It offers an array of fascinating and helpful insights into your life and even your relationships. With astrology, you can explore the positions of stars, planets, and zodiac signs at the time of your birth, or any other person's, and what that could mean. It can help you understand who you are and the possibilities inherent within.

Astrology can give insight into topics like understanding your relationships with others, discovering how energy works in the universe or comprehending the power of the seasons. Not only that, but it can be used as a tool to gain greater self-knowledge and explore life's deeper meanings. Astrology provides many opportunities to find knowledge, rediscover yourself, open your eyes to philosophies beyond the physical world, and see life from new perspectives. Who knows? You may even find astrology enlightening and eye-opening as you search for answers about yourself on this journey.

This detailed guide will explore astrology's foundations, from the planets and signs to the interpretation of your birth chart. It will go over the basics of astrology, such as understanding the meaning behind each planet and sign, finding out what it all means about your birth chart, and more. With each step, you'll better understand this ancient art and how it applies to your life.

Regardless of your knowledge level, this guide will provide the essential understanding and tools to interpret and navigate zodiac signs and everything that relates to it. Come on this journey to explore the skies and unlock the mysteries of astrology!

# Chapter 1: Astrology Basics

In the modern era, astrology may be considered an outdated science. However, throughout human history, it has been used to explain everything from seasonal changes and celestial alignments to life paths and personality traits. Historically, astrological practices originated in India at least four thousand years ago and have since been used by numerous cultures for their own spiritual, religious, and medicinal purposes. The cycles gave them insight into their lives and held important spiritual connotations. Astrological calendars were even used to shape events such as agricultural harvests, military campaigns, and religious ceremonies.

The practice of astrology began in India thousands of years ago. [1]

The shared human love of astrology links people all together, and it's been around since humans developed an understanding of the night sky. Dazzled by the mysteries out there, people tried to make sense of them in ways that still thrill people today. Many ancient civilizations sought answers from the stars and their arrangement in the night sky, from predicting events based on celestial movements to using constellations to create stories. You don't need to believe in astrology to admire its impact on human history.

This chapter will examine how astrology works, the basics of an astrological chart, and the debate of predestination vs. free will. It will then discuss the benefits of astrology, such as understanding personality, unlocking life lessons, gaining insight into life situations, and much more. Finally, it will look at how to interpret an astrological chart and how the interactions between the elements can provide us with life lessons and personality insight.

## Introduction to Astrology

Astrology is an ancient practice that originates in the study of stars and planets and their influence on our lives. By understanding the relationships between various heavenly bodies, astrologers can provide insights into a person's life purpose, issues, successes, and challenges. The consultation process involves understanding the unique situation in a person's life as indicated by planetary motion. Astrology explains different areas of people's lives, from family issues, career paths, and health concerns to everyday attitudes and behaviors. All of this is essentially an attempt to make sense of inexplicable experiences to gain clarity and feel supported in moments of transition or uncertainty. Many people find comfort and guidance in exploring this ancient science. Astrological consults are becoming increasingly popular for people who want insight into life decisions.

## The Basics of an Astrological Chart

An astrological chart is an incredibly powerful tool for looking into the future! It's like a crystal ball made up of mathematical and celestial symbols that can tell you what's ahead in your life. Understanding the basics of an astrological chart will provide insight into areas such as current influences, potential opportunities, and even things that may need extra attention. An astrological chart isn't something to be afraid of; instead, it can be a unique and interesting way to explore life! With a look into your future, who knows what magical surprises await?

## A. Planets

Learning how to read an astrological chart can be a fun way to gain insight into yourself and the world around you. Planets play an essential role in understanding birth charts and predicting the future. Each of the planets has its characteristics, with traditional astrology dividing them into masculine and feminine categories that express respective qualities like reactivity, transformation, and interconnectivity.

Sun signs are a significant factor in determining the traits of a person, while moon signs describe personality on emotional levels. The position of planets regarding each other reveals and activates the energies of that particular birth chart. Using this information, many believe it is possible to get insight into events from daily life to significant milestones. There is still much left to learn about astrology, but exploring the basics of reading a planetary chart provides a great starting point for enlightenment.

## B. Signs

Signs are an essential component of reading an astrological chart. Astrology is a complicated language, with symbols and images representing our universe's different planets and signs. Each sign has its way of expressing itself, which is why understanding the signs can help you gain insight into yourself or others around you. At its core, a chart consists of pictures of circles or squares with labels that determine the sign in question. A chart also highlights aspects such as the expression of energies between each sign and will identify when there will be challenges or benefits during different times. With a deeper understanding of the signs, one can read their birth chart and gain insight into areas such as career, relationships, health, and more.

## C. Houses

Houses in an astrological chart, otherwise known as beams or places, are an integral part of the chart-reading process. They act as lenses, allowing you to focus on specific areas of your life and providing insight into how they correlate to your overall well-being. Each house is associated with particular features such as planets, asteroids, signs, and elements. Studying these powerful indicators allows you to better understand your needs and desires and develop a deeper understanding of yourself and what you need to do to keep yourself healthy and content. If you're curious about the basics of this concept, it's never too late to start exploring. Learning the basics will give you a great foundation for furthering your knowledge from there.

### D. Natal Chart

A natal chart is an astrological representation of a person's date, place, and time of birth. This moment defines and shapes who you are, how you think, and how you will interact with others. It reveals your strengths, weaknesses, gifts, talents, inclinations, and aptitudes. A natal chart can tell you how to approach love and relationships and your career path and even offer insight into life lessons you may learn throughout your lifetime. Although complex, understanding the basics of a natal chart can be empowering and transformational when used as a tool to navigate through life.

## Predestination vs. Free Will

The age-old debate of "predestination versus free will" continues to be explored by theologians and philosophers – even today. On one side, those who believe in predestination argue that man is predetermined to a fate beyond his control. While those with the opposite view believe that our destinies are determined by ourselves and our choices. Both sides of this debate have their merit. While no definite answer has been reached yet, it cannot be denied that exploring this concept can further lead to exciting insights into your purpose in life and how to live it meaningfully.

## Benefits of Astrology

Astrology has a long and rich history, often used by our ancestors to guide daily decisions and bring clarity to the unknown. This science is still relevant today, offering many benefits to those who regularly practice it. Astrology can provide an understanding of ourselves and others by revealing past experiences, their potential for the future, and how certain factors may be influencing them in the present. It goes deeper than just star signs. Astrologers can assess planetary movements, explore zodiac birth charts, numerology cycles, and more to gain personal clarity and develop greater insight into people's lives. In addition, astrology teaches us valuable wisdom, including patience, as we wait for personal cycles to align with cosmic energies. By uncovering this ancient knowledge, you can make lasting improvements in your life and, perhaps most importantly, grow to accept your imperfections!

1. **Understanding Personality**

Astrology is an intriguing ancient practice that still resonates with many people today due to its striking accuracy. It can give you key insights into understanding yourself and your relationships with those around you. Through astrology, you can learn about your personality traits, helping you find the roots of why you think, speak, and behave the way you do. It can also shed light on how different personalities interact with each other, allowing you to create meaningful connections with others and cultivate better relationships. Besides providing valuable self-awareness, by regularly mapping out the movement of planets about your unique zodiac sign, astrology can also alert you to potential opportunities or dangers before they happen, putting you ahead of the game in terms of preparation and action. Regardless of the application, the advantages of utilizing astrology to understand yourself and others are abundantly clear.

2. **Unlocking Life Lessons**

Learning about astrology can be very beneficial in many ways. It can help you become more conscious of appropriate behavior, make you feel more connected to the Universe, and ultimately assist in your personal growth and development. Some may find it fascinating to learn that certain animals, planets, and symbols are associated with their life journey, expanding their knowledge beyond their present lives. Additionally, understanding where the stars stood at the time of birth provides powerful insights into how to interpret their influences on us. With research, practice, consultations, or classes, you can dive into your birth chart, unlocking valuable, insightful messages for guidance in your life. Accessing these life lessons from astrology provides you with guidance and a greater depth of insight that can help you live a happier and more meaningful life.

3. **Gaining Insight into Life Situations**

Unlocking the secrets of astrology can be a great tool for gaining insight into life situations and understanding your relationships with others. Although it's a complex study, some basics like star signs, compatibility charts, and even daily horoscopes are easy to understand. By taking the time to understand what is happening during any given time on the astrological calendar, you can learn more about yourself and gain valuable knowledge of events in your life. Whether predicting potential outcomes or giving advice on navigating tricky circumstances, astrology can be an invaluable resource in our journey of personal growth and self-awareness. With its help, you can discover everything from perfect timing to meaningful messages hidden within life events, truly understanding yourself and your interactions with those around you.

### 4. Strengthening Relationships

Strengthening relationships can be a challenge, but not impossible. Astrology is one tool people find useful to better understand themselves and their partners. It's a fun way to get to know your partner, or yourself, on a deeper level. From introducing some much-needed humor and understanding into conversations to uncovering previously unknown common interests, astrological readings open up pathways for communication between two people that wouldn't have been possible before. It shows you how your unique personality blends in ways you would never have imagined, allowing you to find new depths of connection with others in wonderful ways.

### 5. Discovering Talents and Strengths

Learning about astrology can be an excellent way to discover your talents and strengths. It can provide insight into your inner being, showing which qualities make you unique and which skills you already possess. By exploring the different signs and astrological principles, you may even find that some of your natural talents are unexpected or hidden beneath the surface. Additionally, understanding your strengths can make it easier to turn them into successful career paths or interests. Astrology also offers guidance on how to best use those gifts to explore new ideas, so you can make the most of them with a bit of determination.

### 6. Improving Time Management

Astrology is a powerful tool for improving time management. You know how hard it can be to juggle work, family life, hobbies, and personal health. With astrological guidance, however, you can start to organize the activities you need to do in the right sequence. A great benefit of understanding astrology is synchronizing activities to maximize results. This could mean doing tasks at the most suitable times each day or even designing your week around celestial rhythms that promote productivity. Astrology also refines your ability to prioritize tasks, allowing you to focus on your long-term goals while also addressing smaller tasks' importance. With improved time management skills through astrology, people can live a much more balanced and fulfilled life.

### 7. Promoting Spiritual Growth

Astrology is a great tool for promoting spiritual growth. It offers unique wisdom and insight into your life, personality, and relationships, all of which can help you become more aware of yourself and support your journey of self-discovery. By learning more about the stars, you can gain perspective on your current circumstances, release fear, and understand how to create the life you want. Whether it's getting clarity on an experience or discerning when might be the best time to take action on an important decision, astrology has the insight to guide you toward spiritual growth. With astrology, you can come to a greater understanding of who you are and why you behave in certain ways.

### 8. Improving Decision Making

Making choices and decisions can be difficult, especially when they have long-term implications. It's crucial to make the right decision, and here's where astrology can come in handy! Astrology is an incredible tool for improving decision-making, as it offers insight into your motivations, thoughts, and feelings. Additionally, it helps you gain perspective on your strengths and weaknesses and the possibilities when faced with a complex decision. By examining your astrological chart, you can gain clarity on your current situation and the consequences of certain decisions. Furthermore, astrology offers guidance toward making choices that are best aligned with your goals and desires, allowing you to make conscious decisions instead of blindly going through life without any insight or understanding of your core self. Ultimately, exploring astrological principles is an effective way to support yourself when making sound decisions and living healthier lives.

### 9. Discovering Purpose

Astrology can be a fascinating tool for self-discovery and ultimately fulfilling your purpose in life. With its 12 zodiac signs, astrology helps you to better understand yourself, including your strengths, weaknesses, and inclinations, which allows you to create the path that will bring you closer to your goals. By having an open mind and exploring the position of planets at various stages in your life, you can gain valuable insight into major life decisions like relationships, career moves, or educational pursuits. Believers see what they hope to be as symbols of their destiny in the placement of stars. Skeptics still have the chance to recognize meaning in their lives with knowledge derived from astrological study. Whether you think little or a lot about it, researching astrology may benefit you on your journey to discovering your purpose.

### 10. Moving Towards Fulfillment

In today's world of never-ending decisions, astrology can offer much-needed clarity. There are so many ways it can benefit your life, from uncovering personality traits and life paths to helping you to understand how you interact with certain people or develop relationships. With regular readings and advice tailored to a person's situation or planetary configuration, life decisions can become easier to make. Astrology is designed to provide guidance that ultimately allows room for improvement and growth toward fulfillment in all aspects of your life. Instead of dictating what you should do, it helps you reflect on where you are now, consider the future effects of any decision you may make, and figure out the best way forward for yourself in the long run. Instead of relying on luck or randomness to get you through rough patches in your life, astrology is a great option for finding your path toward true accomplishment and self-growth.

## Interpreting an Astrological Chart

Interpreting an astrological chart can be a complex and bewildering process for the uninitiated. It requires knowledge of planetary interactions, sign representation, and symbolic language interpretation. The task may seem daunting, but it does not need to be. With practice and patience, interpreting astrological charts can become an enlightening tool to expand knowledge and understanding of the cyclical energy patterns in life. Start with smaller charts such as solar returns or daily transits to gain experience, and then progress onto more advanced charts as your confidence and abilities grow. Reach out to friends or online resources if you feel you need guidance. Never underestimate the support available to help you along your journey of unlocking the secrets within the stars.

### A. Interactions between the Elements

Interpreting an astrological chart is an exciting and insightful way to appreciate the interactions between the elements. By studying the placement of planets in the zodiac and the relationships between them, it is possible to gain real insight into one's personality, connections with others, and potential outcomes. Astrology can be a great tool for self-reflection, allowing you to recognize your strengths and weaknesses and appreciate and understand another's perspective to have more meaningful interactions. With an accurate chart and interpretation of its contents, you can get to know yourself much more deeply than you ever thought possible.

### B. Life Lessons and Personality Insight

Interpreting an astrological chart can be a great way to gain more insight into your life and personality. It's a practice that has been used for centuries, and people all around the world continue to use it today. The astrological chart is divided up into twelve houses, each representing different areas of your life such as home life, relationships, career, and more. Each house is connected to planetary placements and aspects that all influence each area. Because of this, examining an astrological chart can give you a better understanding of how those different elements in your life are all interconnected. Instead of just working on changing one isolated aspect of yourself, you can work on simultaneously improving many areas.

### C. How to Interpret Charts in Depth

With the right tools and resources, you can delve into the different elements of a chart to paint a compelling picture of a person or situation. One great way to get started is to learn the language used in astrology to better understand the specific meanings behind each planet and sign. By combining this knowledge with expertise on transits and progressions, house placements, and aspects, individuals can slowly begin to unlock deeper layers of information hidden within their chart. There's so much to uncover when interpreting an astrological chart. With some dedication and practice, you'll soon feel confident interpreting yours!

Astrology readings can be incredibly informative and insightful, opening up avenues of possibilities in our lives. It has been around for centuries, and many people view it as an ancient art form. Interpreting astrological charts involves looking at the alignment of planets within a birth chart or a natal chart to gain insight into someone's essential character traits and life journey. The practice may seem obscure or esoteric, but understanding astrological meaning can help us uncover the hidden potential in ourselves and make sense of our destinies. With the right guide, tools, and resources, it is possible to gain a much deeper understanding of the mysteries of the stars. Dive right in and start deciphering your chart! Who knows what secrets you will uncover?

# Chapter 2: Meet the Astrological Planets

Discovering the energy of the planets and how they can best interact with each astrological house is an exciting journey. All twelve houses have unique properties, so understanding various planetary influences on you can give you a genuinely fascinating insight into your life. The key to benefiting from the information that planets and astrology bring lies in learning the essential components of both fields and seeing which ones come together harmoniously. Learning about the planets' energies will be an invaluable tool for further discoveries.

The planets play an important role in astrology. [2]

This chapter will focus on the role of planets and explore each one in detail. The Sun, Moon, Mercury, Venus, Mars, Jupiter, Saturn, Uranus, Neptune, and Pluto will all be examined. The glyphs associated with each planet will be analyzed, as well as the keywords that best represent them, the deities they're associated with, the zodiac signs ruled by them, and the correspondences (elements, colors, crystals). Finally, a summary of the planet's energy and effects will be provided, so readers can get an idea of how the planet influences their life.

## Understanding the Role of Planets in Astrology

Understanding the role of planets in astrology is a journey that can open your eyes to an entirely new way of looking at the world! As you begin to explore it, you'll discover how each planet symbolizes different qualities and meanings. The Sun, for example, governs the traits associated with one's conscious identity. Mercury is related to intellect and communication; Venus speaks to connection and harmony. Mars signifies energy and ambition. Saturn relates to responsibility and limitations. Jupiter speaks of abundance, growth, and expansiveness. Uranus represents shock, chaos, or a revolution in some aspects of life. Neptune suggests dreams and ephemerality, while Pluto pertains to transformation over time. By introducing yourself to the significance of planets in astrology, you can gain a fascinating insight into yourself as well as those around you on a much deeper level.

## The Sun

The sun is a central figure in the study of astrology, providing you with illuminating insights into your character and behavior. It centers upon what is known as the Sun sign and is determined by where the sun was at the time of your birth. The Sun sign describes our natural dispositions and helps to define who we are. Used in combination with other astrological elements, it can also inform you about how you interact with others, your relationships, and what paths you should follow in life. Knowing your solar influence can be surprisingly helpful when making important decisions. Don't forget to look to the sky and find out what role the sun

Sun glyph. [a]

has to play in your life story!

### A. Glyph Analysis

The glyph representing the sun is a circle with a dot in the center. This symbolizes how your life revolves around the power of this bright star, as it provides humans with energy and light. Additionally, the dot in the center of the circle suggests that within each person lies a special purpose or destiny.

### B. Keywords

Powerful, light, inspiring, energizing, purposeful, illuminating

### C. Associated Deities

Apollo, Ra, Helios, Amaterasu

### D. Zodiac Sign(s) Ruled By It

Leo

### E. Correspondences

- Element: Fire
- Color: Gold or Yellow
- Crystals: Citrine or Tiger's Eye
- Number: 1

### F. Energy and Effects

The sun is a powerful symbol in astrology, representing the light and energy people receive from it. It can provide you with invaluable insights into your character and behavior. Furthermore, it can inform you of how you interact with others, your relationships, and what paths to follow in life. Knowing your solar influence can be a great help when making important decisions.

## The Moon

The role of the Moon in astrology is fascinating and often overlooked. It is believed to be in charge of our energy, instincts, and emotions, and it also influences how people think and behave. When the Moon shifts position or enters a new sign, your way of processing the world changes with it due to its gravitational pull. According to astrologers, studying how the Moon moves through each zodiac sign can help you understand your subconscious responses and any extra intuition about certain topics or situations. Even though Astrology has been looked at with a lot of suspicions over the years, there is something soothing and reassuring about knowing that cosmic energies beyond your control can still positively affect you.

### A. Glyph Analysis

The glyph for the Moon is a crescent shape, reminding us of its connection with tides and natural cycles. It symbolizes your ability to adapt to changing circumstances and your capacity to be open and responsive to the ebb and flow of life.

### B. Keywords

Intuition, emotions, energy, instincts, cycles

### C. Associated Deities

Selene, Diana, Hecate

### D. Zodiac Sign(s) Ruled By It

Cancer

### E. Correspondences

- Element: Water
- Color: Silver or White
- Crystals: Moonstone or Aquamarine
- Number: 2

### F. Energy and Effects

The Moon is an essential figure in astrology. Understanding its influence can provide us with valuable insight into our emotions, intuition, and instincts. The Moon's gravitational pull affects our ability to adapt to new situations. Its movements through the zodiac signs can guide you in your approach to life. Studying and learning about what this cosmic force offers can help you unlock your full potential and live life to the fullest. A more holistic understanding of cosmic energies in your life can make all the difference in making important decisions.

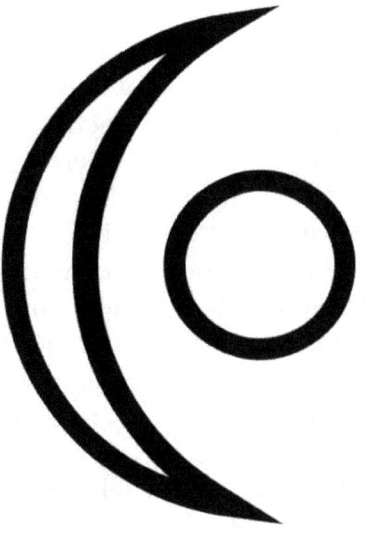

Moon glyph. '

# Mercury

The movements of Mercury are used to interpret a person's behavior, characteristics, and potential future. Mercury represents both logical thought and communication, and knowing this planet can give invaluable insights into how people think and express themselves. It is so influential that it reflects your decisions, values, and behavior as it relates to your relationships with others. Understanding the role of Mercury in astrology can be a powerful tool for understanding yourself and assisting you on your life path.

Mercury glyph.[5]

### A. Glyph Analysis

The glyph for Mercury is a curve above a circle with a cross at the bottom, representing the duality that this planet stands for. It symbolizes your ability to think logically and effectively communicate with others.

### B. Keywords

Communication, intelligence, logic, decisions, relationships

### C. Associated Deities

Mercury, Hermes, Thoth

### D. Zodiac Sign(s) Ruled By It

Gemini and Virgo

### E. Correspondences

- Element: Air
- Color: Orange or Yellow
- Crystals: Citrine or Agate
- Number: 3

### F. Energy and Effects

The movements of Mercury have a significant influence on how you think, behave, and communicate. Its duality is a reminder that your decisions and relationships with others must be balanced for you to live a fulfilling life. Taking the time to understand and learn the effects of Mercury can give you valuable insight into your own life and how you interact with others.

# Venus

As astrology continues to draw in people from all walks of life, the role of Venus stands out as an especially interesting one. Named for the goddess of love and beauty, this planet is believed to govern the areas of love, relationships, and finances. Depending on a person's birth chart, the positioning of Venus can give great insight into an individual's character and destiny. More often than not, it guides them through difficult decisions in their personal lives as they strive to find a balance between their emotional needs and their practical obligations. Knowing more about Venus's influence on our lives can help us make more nuanced decisions that ultimately lead to greater happiness.

Venus glyph.

### A. Glyph Analysis

The glyph for Venus is a circle with a cross at the bottom, representing the feminine energy that this planet brings. It also has an element of balance, as the circle and cross represent a harmonious combination of mental and physical energies.

### B. Keywords

Love, beauty, relationships, finances

### C. Associated Deities

Venus, Aphrodite, Inanna

### D. Zodiac Sign(s) Ruled By It

Taurus and Libra

### E. Correspondences

- Element: Earth
- Color: Green or Pink
- Crystals: Rose Quartz or Jade
- Number: 6

### F. Energy and Effects

Venus governs the areas of love, relationships, and finances. It helps you to find a balance between your emotional needs and practical responsibilities and to make informed decisions about the course your life should take. Understanding how Venus influences you can lead to more meaningful relationships and a greater sense of harmony in your life.

## Mars

When it comes to astrology, the Red Planet Mars is incredibly influential as it has been studied for centuries. This celestial body plays an influential role in a person's zodiac chart and can be used to inform critical life decisions such as travel and career choices. Its energy can also symbolize drive, ambition, and passion, determining how active or determined someone may be. While its malefic aspects are associated with anger or aggression, its positive aspects can bring strength and courage into a person's life. Ultimately, understanding the effects of Mars in astrology can help a person tap into their true potential and take action.

Mars glyph.[7]

### A. Glyph Analysis

The glyph for Mars is a circle with an arrow, indicating the planet's aggressive nature. It is a symbol of strength and courage, which can be directed toward positive or negative outcomes.

### B. Keywords

Action, aggression, ambition, passion

### C. Associated Deities

Mars, Ares, Tyr

### D. Zodiac Sign(s) Ruled By It

Aries and Scorpio

### E. Correspondences

- Element: Fire
- Color: Red
- Crystals: Garnet or Bloodstone
- Number: 4

### F. Energy and Effects

Mars is a powerful and influential planet in astrology, symbolizing drive, ambition, and passion. Taking the time to understand and learn about its effects can help people tap into their true potential and take action to achieve success. With this knowledge, individuals can become more aware of their energy and use it to manifest positive outcomes in all areas of life.

# Jupiter

Jupiter is known as one of the most powerful and influential planets when it comes to astrology. Its role in the solar system goes beyond affecting people's lives. It's essential for the maintenance of a harmonious-balanced collective. When Jupiter goes retrograde, it creates an energetic barrier that deflects difficult energies that can affect your life in unfavorable ways. This acts like a screen that allows you to recognize when you are faced with external and internal challenges. Then, Jupiter acts as a life coach, encouraging you to look within to overcome your obstacles and strengthen your will by reinforcing your motivation. Additionally, because of Jupiter's expansive nature, it also helps increase energy production and general vitality. Therefore, Jupiter plays a major part in maintaining good luck and happiness!

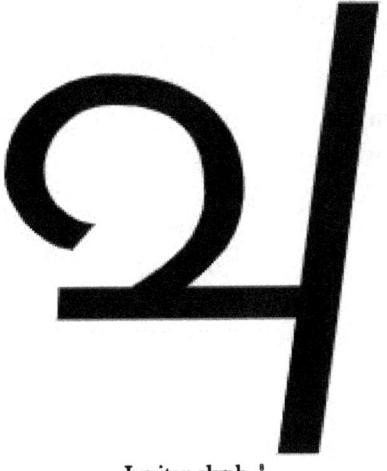

Jupiter glyph.*

### A. Glyph Analysis

The glyph for Jupiter combines two symbols, the crescent moon and the cross. This symbolizes life, growth, expansion, and spiritual and material abundance.

### B. Keywords

Luck, expansion, happiness, growth

### C. Associated Deities

Jupiter, Zeus, Odin

### D. Zodiac Sign(s) Ruled By It
Sagittarius and Pisces

### E. Correspondences
- Element: Fire
- Color: Purple or Blue
- Crystals: Amethyst or Lapis Lazuli
- Number: 3

### F. Energy and Effects

Jupiter is an incredibly influential planet in astrology, symbolizing luck, expansion, happiness, and growth. Its energy can be beneficial when striving for success, and its retrograde periods can even help deflect negative energies. Jupiter encourages you to look within yourself to overcome obstacles and strengthen your will by reinforcing your motivation. Its expansive nature can help you increase your energy production and general vitality and bring more good luck to your life. Ultimately, understanding the effects of Jupiter in astrology can help a person tap into their true potential and achieve success.

## Saturn

Saturn has a special place in astrology, for it rules over time and responsibility. It governs your experience in the physical world, helping you understand when to take action and prioritize tasks. Saturn also challenges you to strive for goals while teaching your soul lessons that force personal growth. Without Saturn's wisdom, you would be unable to move through life with courteous respect for natural law. This can lead to difficulty in experiencing success. With an understanding of the significance of Saturn in astrology, one can learn much about personal progress through timeless knowledge.

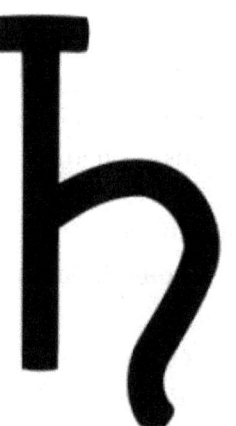

Saturn glyph.

### A. Glyph Analysis

The glyph for Saturn is a cross with a curl at the bottom of it. This symbolizes duty, authority, and limitation, all of which come into play when Saturn is influencing us.

### B. Keywords
Responsibility, structure, wisdom, law

### C. Associated Deities
Saturn, Chronos, Shiva

### D. Zodiac Sign(s) Ruled By It
Capricorn and Aquarius

### E. Correspondences
- Element: Earth
- Color: Black or Gray
- Crystals: Jet or Hematite
- Number: 8

### F. Energy and Effects

Saturn is an important planet in astrology, as it rules over time, responsibility, and authority. It teaches you to be mindful of your actions in life and how best to prioritize tasks. Saturn also encourages you to strive for success while teaching you valuable lessons that can help you grow and develop as an individual. When you understand the significance of Saturn in astrology, you can experience personal progress and benefit from timeless knowledge. With this, you can make conscious choices that bring you closer to your goals and create true success.

## Uranus

Uranus is one of the most intriguing planets in astrology, known for its symbolism of rebellion, disruption, and liberation. Understanding Uranus' key role in any chart can provide valuable insight into a person's spiritual journey, and embracing the lessons associated with the planet can be a powerful source of transformation and growth. Placed within your unique natal birth chart, Uranus brings to light all aspects of your character which are non-conforming. It reveals how you express yourself differently from others and what unconventional paths

Uranus glyph.

you take in your life. Since Uranus rules over innovation, analyzing its placement in your astrological charts helps you understand where your creativity lies and drives you to make meaningful changes.

### A. Glyph Analysis

The glyph for Uranus is two half circles with a cross in the middle. This symbolizes movement, disruption, and liberation from restraints. The symbol contains a circle and cross-shaped elements that illustrate the planet's size and form, an interesting contrast to its colder temperature.

### B. Keywords

Rebellion, disruption, liberation, creativity

### C. Associated Deities

Uranus, Ea, Mithra

### D. Zodiac Sign(s) Ruled By It

Aquarius

### E. Correspondences

- Element: Air
- Color: Blue or Turquoise
- Crystals: Aquamarine or Tourmaline
- Number: 7

### F. Energy and Effects

Uranus is one of the most interesting planets in astrology, known for its symbolism of rebellion, disruption, and liberation. Its placement in your astrological charts can help you understand your creative side and how to express yourself differently from others. Uranus teaches you to break free from restraints and embrace unconventional paths in life, which can lead to meaningful changes. With an understanding of the significance of Uranus in astrology, one can learn a lot about personal growth and transformation.

# Neptune

Neptune is an intriguing planet within astrology, as it has been known to bring spiritual growth and higher consciousness. By understanding Neptune's role in astrology, you can use this knowledge to better understand yourself and your place in the universe. Specifically, Neptune's presence relates to your subconscious mind and its relation to dreams, creativity, and imagination. When you understand the power of Neptune, you can acknowledge that each person has access to the remarkable potential for spiritual transcendence and new understanding. Exploring Neptune's influence is a fascinating journey of self-discovery that may lead you to uncover hidden insights about yourself that have immense power for transformation!

Neptune glyph. [10]

## A. Glyph Analysis

The glyph for Neptune is a trident, an ancient symbol of authority and power. The trident also represents three prongs that represent the three aspects of Neptune, including spirituality, creativity, and imagination.

## B. Keywords

Mysterious, spiritual, creative, imaginative

## C. Associated Deities

Neptune, Poseidon, Manannan Mac Lir

## D. Zodiac Sign(s) Ruled By It

Pisces

## E. Correspondences

- Element: Water
- Color: Blue or Purple
- Crystals: Moonstone or Amethyst
- Number: 8

## F. Energy and Effects

Neptune is astrology's powerful and mysterious planet, often associated with spiritual growth and higher consciousness. Analyzing Neptune's role in your astrological chart can help you to understand your subconscious mind and its influence on your dreams, creativity, and imagination. By understanding Neptune's significance in astrology, you can access tremendous potential for spiritual transcendence and unlock new insights about yourself that can transform your life.

# Pluto

As a small, distant planet in Earth's solar system, Pluto has often been overlooked in astrology. However, that's no longer the case. As an outer planet, Pluto can have a strong influence on you. It often signifies transformation and momentous life changes. Astrological interpretations suggest that Pluto represents one's ability to dig deep into their truth and innermost desires. By understanding Pluto's symbolism, you can gain insight into your maturity. The energy of this planet can guide powerful discoveries within ourselves, from breaking old habits and misconceptions to embracing who we truly are.

Pluto glyph.

### A. Glyph Analysis

The glyph for Pluto is a small circle with a cross underneath it, symbolizing the planet's deep and mysterious nature. The circle represents unity, while the cross suggests transformation, composed of two intersecting lines representing different directions.

### B. Keywords

Mysterious, transformative, powerful, intense

### C. Associated Deities

Pluto, Demeter, Hades

### D. Zodiac Sign(s) Ruled by It

Scorpio

### E. Correspondences

- Element: Water
- Color: Black
- Crystals: Obsidian or Jet
- Number: 8

### F. Energy and Effects

Pluto is a small, distant planet in the solar system that often signifies transformation and momentous life changes. By understanding Pluto's symbolism, you can gain insight into your maturity. Exploring the energy of this planet can guide powerful discoveries within yourself and can help you to break old habits and misconceptions and embrace who you truly are.

In conclusion, the planets (Sun, Moon, Mercury, Venus, Mars, Jupiter, Saturn, Uranus, Neptune, and Pluto) of astrology each have their special energy and influence the lives of individuals in unique ways. By exploring these planets, you can gain valuable insight into your personal growth and development. By understanding each planet's symbolism, you can unlock hidden truths about yourself and use that knowledge to create meaningful change in your life.

# Chapter 3: Nodes and Asteroids Matter, Too

The core mechanics of astrology can often be drilled down to the influence of the planets. They shine a light on personality traits, relational interactions, and much more. While these celestial bodies are majorly responsible for defining the energies that shape you astrologically, there are minor energies that shouldn't be overlooked. Asteroids and nodes complete an intricate cosmic puzzle that helps you to fully understand yourself. The asteroids often depict your innermost emotions and relationships, while the nodes provide hidden influences or behaviors that are still impactful.

Asteroids play a role in astrological readings. [11]

Astrology relies on major and minor energies to gain a clear picture of your life or even past lives that you can look into for deeper understanding. These energies come together to create something personal, an in-depth reading that provides insight into who you are and what potential paths exist in front of you. It's an interesting way to reflect on ourselves and find solace in discovering the unique beauty that comes from your cosmic origins.

This chapter will explore two of astrology's most important minor energies, including asteroids and the nodes. It will break down their meanings and roles in your life, explain how they can affect you, what lessons they teach, and how they work together to create a complete picture of your life. By the end of this chapter, you will better understand the importance of minor energies in astrology and how they can be used to help you make better decisions.

## Nodes

Astrology can be an interesting and complex field to study. In astrology, Nodes refer to the North and South Node, which represent your Karmic past and where your soul is heading. By determining the location of the Nodes in our birth chart, one can learn more about their past life influences and their place in their current journey. Studying nodes in astrology can shed light on how we're creating or manifesting certain aspects of our life, so it can be a great learning tool for anyone looking to gain a deeper understanding of their own lives. Also, exploring astrological nodes helps you learn more about why you are drawn to some people and repelled by others or why some situations attract you while others turn you off. Overall, it's a great exercise in self-discovery, and there is so much to discover!

### A. Definition of Nodes

The nodes in astrology are two very specific points on the celestial sphere representing a philosophical clash between one's past, present, and future. The north node represents the most beneficial path for you to follow, and the south node represents lessons from your experiences. They are not planets or signs. They are mathematical points that provide insight into your life to maximize your potential and better understand your dilemmas and challenges. Every cycle of the nodes around the chart takes roughly eighteen months, making it an incredibly powerful tool when studying personal growth and collective shifts. Of course, astrology is not limited to just these two points. Still, it can provide you with incredible insight into your spiritual and material pursuits.

### B. South Node

Have you ever heard of the South Node in Astrology? This critical concept is about looking into your past and unpacking how past experiences shape you today. The South Node relates to where you come from on your spiritual journeys, and it speaks to who you were before this current life. As the astrological sign closest to the body's energy field, the South Node can tell you about previous karmic patterns, such as beliefs, feelings, and expectations that may be holding you back from achieving future goals. It is truly an intriguing concept that is well worth exploring if you want to understand yourself or those around you on a deeper level.

### C. North Node

Understanding your North Node in astrology can be a fascinating journey. It requires looking back at the past, delving into your story, and coming up with a fresh perspective. Your North Node is believed to be connected to your destiny and the highest realization of yourself. Consider this equivalent to your zodiac's version of a flight plan. Understanding it could provide invaluable insight into who you are and where you're headed. It could also help with making difficult decisions on what new beginnings will align with your higher purpose. Take some time for deeper exploration and reflect on how your North Node lessons might help you find more joy and fulfillment in life.

### D. Role of Black Moon Lilith

In the world of Astrology, Black Moon Lilith is an incredibly influential figure. This mysterious object can reveal vital insights into your life and your relationships with others, including its effects on you both individually and collectively. Lilith represents the more shadowy sides of your soul, such as dark energy, self-sabotage, self-destructive behaviors, repressed desires, and even trauma that has been left unresolved. But it can also point to your capacity for transformative growth and strength. Taking the time to understand your own Black Moon Lilith opens up a whole new realm of possibilities for personal insight, healing, and growth in life.

# Asteroids

For many people, asteroids can be fascinating petite planets that provide enigmatic messages about our destinies. They play an essential role in astrology, as the individual patterns formed by the configuration of asteroids in your chart reveal hidden insights. Looking at asteroid astrology provides a roadmap to understanding certain events and behaviors in your life. Every placement lets you delve deeper into who you are and where you are heading. From Juno revealing where commitment comes from to Chiron connecting us to past soul wounds and Ceres helping you find patterns within both positive and negative experiences, asteroids give you intricate knowledge about life's many mysteries.

## Chiron

The mighty asteroid of Chiron has long been a source of interest for astrologers. Commonly known as the "wounded healer" due to its unpredictable and paradoxical nature, it is believed to represent your capacity for compassion and understanding. This asteroid helps you understand your life's purpose and thus better plan for your life moving forward. It also has great symbolic meaning in terms of showing how you can rise above the suffering in your life, regardless of its form or intensity. As such, astrologers often look towards this ancient celestial body when interpreting the stars and gaining insight into your experiences. With its unique interpretation, Chiron is truly a special asteroid with deep connections within astrology.

### A. Glyph Analysis

After analyzing its glyph, it appears that the "C" shape indicates energy circulation within the solar system, while the two main lines represent the sun-earth relationship. The glyph also includes a symbol pointing toward our place in this phenomenon. This symbolic representation teaches you to be aware of your role as a part of a much bigger systemic structure and reminds you to be mindful of how you interact with it.

### B. Keywords

Transformation, growth, healing

### C. Associated Deities

Apollo, Artemis, Hecate, Prometheus, Hygeia

### D. Zodiac Sign(s) Ruled By It
Aries, Leo, Sagittarius

### E. Correspondences
- Element: Fire
- Color: Gold
- Crystals: Amethyst, Moonstone
- Number: 9

### F. Energy and Effects

Chiron is an asteroid associated with transformation, growth, healing, and understanding. It has a powerful impact on the energy of those it influences and empowers them to make changes in their lives. It can offer insight into the purpose of suffering and how your wounds can be used to create something beautiful. By connecting to its energy, you can better understand your destinies and find the strength to overcome any obstacles. Ultimately, Chiron reminds you to let go of the past, embrace your wounds, and use them to keep growing.

## Ceres

What is the astrological significance of the dwarf planet Ceres? This is a question that has been asked by many throughout history. It turns out that this asteroid has an important role to play in the cosmos, with particular relevance for individuals who follow astrology. From its place within the solar system, Ceres is thought to influence your life and contribute to a balance between your nature, growth, and nourishment. Studying this asteroid can give you greater insight into yourself and your purpose here on Earth. For those interested in taking a deeper look, researching how our relationship with this celestial body influences our relationships with others can be enlightening.

### A. Glyph Analysis

The glyph of Ceres is composed of two circles, with a cross in the center, representing fertility and nourishment. The circles represent the earth, while the cross in the center suggests that all living things are connected. This glyph is also symbolic of Ceres' role as a guardian and caretaker of the Earth by providing sustenance to all living things.

### B. Keywords

Abundance, nurture, fertility, motherhood

### C. Associated Deities
Demeter, Aphrodite, Persephone, Cybele

### D. Zodiac Sign(s) Ruled By It
Taurus, Virgo, Capricorn

### E. Correspondences
- Element: Earth
- Color: Green
- Crystals: Chrysoprase, Jade
- Number: 5

### F. Energy and Effects
Ceres is an asteroid associated with abundance, nurture, fertility, and motherhood. It is believed to strongly influence your relationships with other people and your environment. By connecting to its energy, you can better understand your identity and purpose in life. It encourages you to be more nurturing, compassionate, and generous toward yourself and those around you. Ultimately, Ceres reminds you to take care of yourself and those close to you, so you can be the best version of yourself.

# Pallas

Astrologers have long been intrigued by the mysterious Pallas asteroid because of its close relationship with your innermost thoughts as it relates to self-mastery and wisdom. Symbolically, this asteroid carries metaphysical insight into how you act in the world. It is believed that understanding your directive, purpose, and motivation can help you grow spiritually and even break old patterns of behavior which impede your progress. Although the Pallas asteroid speaks mostly to the deeper spiritual aspects within everyone, it also speaks to the outer environment since several myths include it as a symbol of protection against enemies, both hidden and obvious. Finally, because of its connection to wisdom, astrologers often look to its insights when trying to unravel tough life issues such as relationships or career decisions.

### A. Glyph Analysis
The glyph of Pallas is composed of a shield and spear, representing protection and strength. It suggests that Pallas plays an essential role in guarding people against their enemies by providing them with the wisdom and bravery to overcome obstacles.

### B. Keywords
Protection, strength, wisdom, strategy

### C. Associated Deities
Athena, Minerva, Nike

### D. Zodiac Sign(s) Ruled By It
Aquarius, Libra

### E. Correspondences
- Element: Air
- Color: Silver
- Crystals: Hematite, Jet
- Number: 8

### F. Energy and Effects
Pallas is an asteroid that helps you be mindful of how you act and understand your role. Its energy can give you strength, courage, and confidence to take on the challenges that come your way and make decisions with clarity and purpose. By connecting to its energy, you can gain greater insight into your life's direction and increase your chances of success in your endeavors. Pallas reminds you to trust yourself and step out of your comfort zone to reach your highest potential. It encourages you to use strategy and wisdom to protect yourself against any kind of external or internal enemies.

# Juno

Juno is an asteroid that has been coming into focus lately, particularly due to its relation to astrology. Named for the Roman goddess of marriage and romance, Juno is seen as a significant symbol amongst stargazers, carrying messages of partnership and devotion. Astrologers across the globe have attributed different meanings to it, from exploring heartbreak, and honoring female principles, to creating profound unions with other individuals (relationships that result in stability and delight). Its discovery adds insight into the many mysteries of the skies, thought-provoking and captivating. The sight of Juno in a person's natal chart may excite or spark caution, depending on how it's perceived, leading you to look deeper into how love shows up in your life.

### A. Glyph Analysis

The glyph of Juno is a triangular shape, with two open and one closed side. This signifies the mixed bag of emotions that come along with love and relationships, showing the balance between openness and protection when it comes to partnership.

### B. Keywords

Love, marriage, commitment, union, relationship

### C. Associated Deities

Juno, Venus

### D. Zodiac Sign(s) Ruled By It

Taurus, Libra

### E. Correspondences

- Element: Earth
- Color: Red and Pink
- Crystals: Rose Quartz, Rhodonite
- Number: 6

### F. Energy and Effects

Juno's energy encourages you to explore how to approach relationships and find joy and fulfillment in your partnerships. It can create an awareness of the importance of commitment, responsibility, and trust in any relationship dynamic. Juno's energy can allow you to create deeper connections with those closest to you and encourages you to operate from a place of love instead of fear. It teaches you to take a stand for your own needs while still allowing you to be open and vulnerable. Juno encourages you to focus on the basic needs of partnership and to find strength in your relationship bonds. By connecting with its energy, you can create an atmosphere of mutual respect and understanding, allowing you to create loving and lasting unions.

## Vesta

Astrology enthusiasts have a new source of fascination in the Vesta asteroid, considered to be the brightest object in the asteroid belt. Discovered by German astronomer Heinrich Olbers in 1807, it is thought to represent Virgo, the Virgin Maiden of ancient goddess myths. Those who think your destiny is written in the stars believe Vesta's influence could bring clarity and help achieve goals with minimal effort. Other astrological interpretations suggest that it can enhance sexual relationships, family life, and feelings of camaraderie. Regardless of what path you choose to explore or how you interpret Vesta's influence on your life, its magnetism will surely take you on an interesting journey!

### A. Glyph Analysis

The glyph for Vesta is two intersecting circles, representing the union of spiritual and physical energies. It also symbolizes the combination of material and spiritual gifts that we, as individuals, can use to reach our highest potential.

### B. Keywords

Focused, dedicated, devoted, passionate, disciplined

### C. Associated Deities

Vesta, Hestia, Athena

### D. Zodiac Sign(s) Ruled By It

Virgo

### E. Correspondences

- Element: Earth
- Color: White and Silver
- Crystals: Rock Crystal, Obsidian
- Number: 5

### F. Energy and Effects

Vesta's energy encourages you to remain devoted and passionate about what matters most to you. It helps you to stay focused and remember the importance of your dedication, even when faced with obstacles or setbacks. This energy can inspire feelings of security and trust within relationships and a sense of camaraderie or "team spirit." Vesta can help you stay devoted to your goals, dreams, and ambitions in life. Its energy can also bring a sense of balance and harmony to any situation, allowing you to stay true to yourself and your values. When you tap into the power of Vesta, you can remain disciplined and passionate about your pursuits while still being gentle and understanding toward others.

# Eros

Astronomers worldwide are highly familiar with Eros Asteroid, a celestial body renowned for its cosmic significance. It is believed to influence individuals based on their birth date, helping to provide a glimpse at what can be expected in their lives. This very special celestial body interacts with the most personal parts of our natal chart and transmits amazing energy that can help you to soar or falter, depending on how it's activated. Astrologers look at the many aspects of Eros Asteroid to gain insights into what's happening both inside and outside an individual. From facing forces within yourself, understanding your desires, improving communication skills, and finding the right kind of love, Eros has a mix of various elements that make it truly unique. Its effects feel like nothing else, providing you with a powerful force to explore yourself more deeply.

### A. Glyph Analysis

The glyph for Eros is a circle with an arrow pointing downward. This symbolizes the powerful and passionate energy of love and the ability to penetrate and open up what had previously been closed off.

### B. Keywords

Romance, passion, intimacy, desire, sensuality

### C. Associated Deities

Eros, Aphrodite, Cupid

### D. Zodiac Sign(s) Ruled By It

Taurus, Libra

### E. Correspondences

- Element: Water
- Color: Red and Pink
- Crystals: Rose Quartz, Garnet
- Number: 7

### F. Energy and Effects

Eros is the god of love, passion, and intimacy. His energy helps you open your heart and find the courage to express yourself authentically in relationships. It encourages you to take risks and embrace your desires while giving you the courage to explore new avenues. This energy can help you access a deeper connection with yourself and others, allowing you to break free from your inhibitions and discover a passion for life. Eros also helps you open up to the healing power of love and experience the joys of intimate relationships. With his energy, you can deepen your understanding of yourself and others and find the courage to take risks and explore your passions.

# Hygeia

Hygeia, or asteroid 10, is one of the largest asteroids in the Solar System and has been thought to have a powerful influence on astrology. Named after the Greek goddess of health, Hygeia was discovered in 1854 and has since become a powerhouse for understanding our psychological nature. People look into their natal chart right around the placement of Hygeia to find greater clarity about health issues that could be affecting their life journey and how they can better care for themselves. The asteroid symbolizes prevention, healthy boundaries, and good habits, so it can help people take back control over their well-being. Plus, with all its links to mystical forces that are beyond our understanding, learning more about Hygeia can be quite an adventure.

### A. Glyph Analysis

The glyph for Hygeia is a bowl with a serpent wrapped around it. This symbolizes the protection, healing, and nourishment that Hygeia can provide. It also represents the need for boundaries and limits in life, as well as our ability to take care of ourselves in a holistic way.

### B. Keywords

Health, self-care, protection, boundaries, limits

### C. Associated Deities

Hygeia, Asclepius

### D. Zodiac Sign(s) Ruled By It

Virgo

### E. Correspondences

- Element: Earth
- Color: Green and Yellow
- Crystals: Jade, Chrysocolla, Tiger's Eye
- Number: 9

## F. Energy and Effects

Hygeia's energy encourages us to care for our physical and emotional health by setting boundaries and limits. It helps you find healing in your body, mind, and spirit and teaches you to look after yourself holistically. This energy also emphasizes the importance of understanding your limits and having the courage to set them to be able to enjoy a healthy lifestyle. Hygeia's energy encourages you to be vigilant in your self-care and preventative health while helping you recognize your need for boundaries. Finally, this energy teaches you to listen to your body and respect its warnings to stay healthy. Hygeia's energy helps you become more knowledgeable and aware of your well-being, making your best choices.

Astrology is an incredible science for interpreting the subtle messages of the zodiac and gaining insight into your life. Two significant sources astrologers use to understand the stars are asteroids and nodes. Asteroids offer a detailed interpretation of your relationship with others and your world, while nodes signify important turning points in your life journey. Together, these cosmic elements bring a deeper perspective to the meanings behind your zodiac sign. Studying these powerful tools can be incredibly rewarding as you explore the often mysterious language of the cosmos.

# Chapter 4: The 12 Zodiac Signs

Zodiac signs allow you to glimpse the magnificence of the cosmos by providing insight into how the energy of planets, asteroids, and nodes in the solar systems affect people. Each sign corresponds with its unique influences, affecting different areas of your life, such as your personality, relationships, and lifestyle choices. By learning the different

The zodiac wheel. [13]

traits associated with each sign, you can learn more about yourself and apply this information to make better decisions for living a fulfilling life. Consulting astrological forecasts based on your zodiac sign can unlock greater wisdom and understanding that you never knew existed. It's like opening the door to an entirely new perspective.

This chapter will explore the significance of each sign in depth. Starting with a brief overview of the wheel of zodiac signs, it will then delve into examining each sign in detail, from the meaning behind its glyph and symbol through to the introduction of its ruling planet, as well as other correspondences (such as color, metal, stone, and body part). By the end of this chapter, you will have a better idea of what each sign brings to the table and how it shapes your life and character.

Whether you believe in astrology or not, there's a fascinating beauty to the wheel of stars and planets that spells out a possible destiny from birth. Each sign has its characteristics and traits associated with it, ranging from the bubbly Aries to the responsible Capricorn. At this wheel of fate, you can get to know yourself better, find those around you easier to understand, jumpstart your creativity, and even achieve a more peaceful temperament. It won't give you exact answers, but it will help you make better choices on your journey through life.

## A Closer Look at Each Sign

Learning about the different zodiac signs can be incredibly enlightening and surprisingly accurate! Zodiac signs are based on the Earth's cycles, as seen through classical astrology. They aim to provide insight into your personality, motivation, and interactions with others. Begin by familiarizing yourself with each zodiac sign's unique characteristics, from Aries' adventurousness to Pisces' sensitivity. You can then explore your sign's compatibility with others or dive deeper into how each interacts differently with relationships, career paths, and more. Get ready to explore this fascinating world. Who knows what you will find out about yourself?

## Aries (March 21–April 19)

Those born between March 21 and April 19 will most likely have a fiery temper and an eager attitude to match their Zodiac sign, Aries. No task is too challenging for this determined sign, which also means that Aries natives usually don't take no for an answer. They'll rightly focus their incredible energy on what makes them truly passionate. They also remain level-headed when it comes to anything else. An Aries will often take the initiative in matters where others lack motivation or are unwilling to take action. If you're looking for someone who won't back down and can give it their all in any situation, then an Aries might just be the perfect fit.

### A. Glyph and Symbol

The glyph of Aries is that of a ram's horns, while the symbol is a ram itself. Both represent the sign's determination and willingness to go above and beyond for success. This can describe their unwavering nature and the courage and determination they exhibit when faced with a challenge.

### B. Keywords

Courageous, Energetic, Determined

### C. Element

Aries is a Fire sign, and its element is Fire, which represents passion and enthusiasm. This zodiac sign is all about action and taking the initiative, which explains why they often seem unstoppable.

### D. Modality

Aries is a cardinal sign, meaning they usually lead with enthusiasm and eagerness to try new things. They are not afraid of taking risks or being the first to take a leap of faith.

### E. Planet

Mars is the ruling planet of Aries, and its influence can be seen in the native's fiery temper and strong-willed nature.

### F. Polarity

Aries is a positive sign, meaning they tend to be optimistic, focused, and determined in their approach.

### G. Correspondences

- Color: Red
- Metal: Iron
- Stone: Diamond
- Body Part: Head and face.

## Taurus (April 20–May 20)

The Taurus sign is associated with stability, firmness, and dependability, essential traits in life's most important relationships. Ruled by Venus, the planet of beauty and love, these zodiac lovers prefer comfort and security in all their endeavors. The earth element of Taurus gives them an affinity for nature, which often leads to a penchant for home comforts and a slow-paced lifestyle. They like their lives to move at a leisurely pace, allowing them sufficient time to enjoy the finer things in life. Those born under this star sign possess great perseverance and determination, with strong intuitions to guide their decisions. Sensual by nature, Taurus is romantic, devoted, and faithful, which makes them fantastic friends and partners.

### A. Glyph and Symbol

The glyph of Taurus is the bull's head, while its symbol is a bull. These represent the sign's strong will and determination, as well as its loyalty to loved ones and its tendency to remain steadfast.

### B. Keywords

Stable, Dependable, Loyal

### C. Element

Taurus is an Earth sign, and its element is Earth which symbolizes stability and reliability. This zodiac sign is all about slow-paced stability, preferring to take their time when making decisions.

### D. Modality

Taurus is a fixed sign, meaning they are focused and determined to stay true to their goals and values. They have unshakable confidence in their convictions and won't waver even when faced with adversity.

### E. Planet

Venus is the ruling planet of Taurus, and its influence can be seen in the sign's appreciation for beauty and love. They tend to be romantic, devoted, and faithful, making them fantastic friends and companions.

### F. Polarity

Taurus is a positive sign, meaning they tend to be optimistic and focused on their goals. They have a strong will and determination that allow them to stay true to their convictions no matter what.

### G. Correspondences

- Color: Green
- Metal: Copper
- Stone: Emerald
- Body Part: Throat and neck.

# Gemini (May 21–June 21)

Gemini is the ultimate chameleon. Changeable and versatile, they can fit in with any group of people regardless of their background. Gemini people are born to communicate, often speaking with a natural flair that is sure to captivate those around them. They have encyclopedic knowledge stored up in their head, so don't be surprised if you find yourself getting lost in conversation with one. Their open-mindedness and curiosity drive them to learn more about the world and seek out stimulating new experiences. All these things come together to make Geminis truly rewarding friends who are sure to bring plenty of joy into your life.

### A. Glyph and Symbol

The glyph of Gemini is two crescent moons, while its symbol is the twins. This symbolizes the sign's dual nature and its ability to adapt to any situation.

### B. Keywords

Adaptable, Versatile, Intelligent

### C. Element

Gemini is an Air sign that symbolizes the sign's need for intellectual stimulation and the ability to think quickly. It is associated with communication, ideas, and creativity.

### D. Modality

Gemini is a Mutable sign, which means it is flexible and open to change. They have a knack for adapting to any situation and can easily switch between different tasks.

### E. Planet

Mercury is the ruling planet of Gemini. Its influence can be seen in the sign's keen intellect and excellent communication skills.

### F. Polarity

Gemini is a positive sign, meaning that they are optimistic and open-minded. They can easily adapt to any situation, and their enthusiasm and energy can bring plenty of joy into your life.

### G. Correspondences

- Color: Yellow
- Metal: Mercury
- Stone: Agate
- Body Part: Arms and hands.

# Cancer (June 22–July 22)

The Cancer zodiac sign is known for its compassion and thoughtfulness. People born under the Cancer sign are often considered to be intuitive with a great capacity for understanding others. They strive to make everyone around them feel secure and emotionally cared for. These qualities, combined with their strong survival skills, make them an asset in any team project. In relationships, Cancers tend to be loyal, devoted, and protective of those they love. Although they may become moody or reclusive at times, they demonstrate incredible strength and resilience regarding life's biggest challenges.

### A. Glyph and Symbol

The glyph of Cancer is the crab, while its symbol is the Crab's claw. This symbolizes the sign's ability to protect and nurture those it loves.

### B. Keywords

Loyal, Nurturing, Protective

### C. Element

Cancer is a Water sign that symbolizes the sign's strong emotional nature and the need for security and stability. It is associated with empathy, sensitivity, and intuition.

### D. Modality

Cancer is a Cardinal sign which means that the sign is driven and goal-oriented. They are motivated to take the initiative and get things done, no matter the challenge.

### E. Planet

The Moon is the ruling planet of Cancer. Its influence can be seen in the sign's strong emotional nature and need for security.

### F. Polarity

Cancer is a negative sign, meaning that they are introspective and empathetic. They are devoted to their loved ones and strive to create a safe and secure environment for them.

### G. Correspondences

- Color: Silver
- Metal: Moon
- Stone: Moonstone
- Body Part: Chest and stomach.

# Leo (July 23–August 22)

Leo is a fire sign, which means its symbolization is greatly inspired by the sun. Leos strive for success and energy, aiming to be noticed and recognized. People under this sign are born with leadership traits that allow them to succeed in almost any path they choose in life. They are always willing to try something new, always looking for something that fulfills their need for creativity. This is an inspiring sign of persistence and courage that never fails to draw the attention of others. Generally speaking, Leos will always stand out from the crowd because of their generous nature and positive attitude. No wonder it's considered one of the strongest zodiac signs around.

### A. Glyph and Symbol

The glyph of Leo is the Lion, while its symbol is a lion's head. This symbolizes the sign's strong nature, as well as its leadership traits.

### B. Keywords

Generous, Energetic, Confident

### C. Element

Leo is a Fire sign symbolizing the sign's strong will and passion. It is associated with strength, enthusiasm, and creativity.

### D. Modality

Leo is a fixed sign which means that the sign is reliable, focused, and hard-working. They are determined to finish what they start and never give up on their goals.

### E. Planet

The Sun is the ruling planet of Leo, and its influence can be seen in the sign's strong drive and ambition.

### F. Polarity

Leo is a positive sign, meaning that they are confident and passionate. They are generous and optimistic, always striving to improve the world.

### G. Correspondences

- Color: Gold
- Metal: Sun
- Stone: Ruby
- Body Part: Heart and spine.

# Virgo (August 23–September 22)

If you're born between August 23 and September 22, then you are a Virgo. Virgos tend to be very analytical and detail-oriented, making great executives or problem solvers. They also value ethics and treat others with respect. It is not uncommon for them to dream big but take measured steps to reach their goals. Their organizational skills mean that they excel at anything requiring precision and attention to detail, while their perception helps them understand the workings of the world around them. Although they may come across as perfectionists, deep down, they are generally compassionate souls who deeply care about lifestyle improvement and the welfare of their close friends and family. Overall, having a Virgo in your life is a rewarding experience. You'll have a loyal friend for life if you earn their trust.

### A. Glyph and Symbol

The glyph of Virgo is the Maiden, while its symbol is a Virgin woman. This symbolizes the sign's purity and innocence.

### B. Keywords

Analytical, Detail-oriented, Ethical

### C. Element

Virgo is an Earth sign which symbolizes the sign's practicality and stability. It is associated with structure, grounding, and productivity.

### D. Modality

Virgo is a Mutable sign which means that the sign is adaptable, flexible, and open-minded. They can easily take on new tasks and change directions if needed.

### E. Planet

The ruling planet of Virgo is Mercury, and its influence can be seen in the sign's analytical mind and love of communication.

### F. Polarity

Virgo is a Negative sign, meaning they tend to be more introverted and concerned with the details. They are focused on improving themselves rather than relying on external sources.

### G. Correspondences

- Color: Silver
- Metal: Mercury
- Stone: Peridot
- Body Part: Intestinal system.

# Libra (September 23–October 23)

Libra is an air sign, which means creativity and intellectual curiosity are at the core of their being. People born under the Libra zodiac sign have an innate sense of balance and harmony, making them great problem-solvers and peacemakers. They are strikingly social creatures whose charm puts people at ease, friends, acquaintances, and strangers alike because they can always see different sides of complex situations or problems. Whether they can easily organize parties or just have a good time, Libras are sure to make any event more enjoyable. Ultimately, nothing matters more to this sign than finding balance in all areas of life, including work, play, and relationships.

### A. Glyph and Symbol

The glyph of Libra is the Scales, while its symbol is a pair of scales balanced between two horizontal lines. This symbolizes the sign's search for balance and justice in all aspects of life.

### B. Keywords

Social, Harmonious, Balanced

### C. Element

Libra is an Air sign which symbolizes the sign's intellectual curiosity and creativity. It is associated with communication, knowledge, and connecting ideas.

### D. Modality

Libra is a Cardinal sign which means that the sign is a natural leader who can take charge and motivate others. They are driven to succeed, but their sense of justice prevents them from taking shortcuts.

### E. Planet

The ruling planet of Libra is Venus, and its influence can be seen in the sign's charm and beauty.

### F. Polarity

Libra is a Positive sign, meaning that they naturally strive for harmony in all areas of life. They are focused on connecting with others instead of relying on internal sources.

### G. Correspondences

- Color: Pastel Blue
- Metal: Copper
- Stone: Opal
- Body Part: Lower Back.

# Scorpio (October 24–November 21)

Scorpios are known for being passionate, intense, and intuitive people. These qualities make them great leaders. Those born under Scorpio live life with a strong sense of power and purpose. This can manifest in their deep insights and understanding, often seeing into the heart of a problem or situation more quickly than others. They also have an unyielding determination for success coupled with an uncanny ability to adapt through challenging times that helps them reach their goals. With this combination of qualities, it should be no surprise that they often find themselves leaders in most of their chosen endeavors. If you know someone born under this star sign, be sure to appreciate them and all they bring to the table.

### A. Glyph and Symbol

The glyph of Scorpio is a Scorpion with its tail pointing downward, symbolizing the sign's ability to strike with precision and accuracy. Its symbol is the same.

### B. Keywords

Powerful, Intense, Adaptable

### C. Element

Scorpio is a Water sign which symbolizes their strong intuition and emotional depth. It is associated with feelings, emotions, and the collective unconscious.

### D. Modality

Scorpio is a fixed sign which means that the sign is focused on finding strength and stability in their lives. They are loyal to those they love and tenacious in their pursuits, never giving up until they find their desired outcome.

### E. Planet

The ruling planet of Scorpio is Mars, and its influence can be seen in the sign's courage and determination.

### F. Polarity

Scorpio is a Negative sign, meaning they are more focused on internal sources of power than external ones.

### G. Correspondences

- Color: Dark Red
- Metal: Steel
- Stone: Topaz
- Body Part: Reproductive Organs.

# Sagittarius (November 22–December 21)

Sagittarians are known for having energetic personalities, open-mindedness, and bravery. They have something unique to offer the world: they fearlessly express their inner truths through their curious minds and enthusiasm. Plus, they make great friends since they're funny and fun to be around. So, if you know a Sagittarius (or are one!), prepare for plenty of adventure, new experiences, and interesting conversations.

### A. Glyph and Symbol

The glyph of Sagittarius is an Archer with its bow and arrow pointing up, symbolizing the sign's aim for success and its eagerness to explore new territory. Its symbol is the same.

### B. Keywords

Energetic, Open-Minded, Brave

### C. Element

Sagittarius is a Fire sign which symbolizes their natural passion and enthusiasm. It is associated with action, drive, and creative expression.

### D. Modality

Sagittarius is a Mutable sign which means that the sign is focused on change, growth, and transformation. They adapt to their environment and always seek ways to expand their understanding of the world.

### E. Planet

The ruling planet of Sagittarius is Jupiter, and its influence can be seen in the sign's optimism, faith, and expansive nature.

### F. Polarity

Sagittarius is a Positive sign, meaning that they focus more on external sources of power than internal ones.

### G. Correspondences

- Color: Light Blue
- Metal: Tin
- Stone: Turquoise
- Body Part: Hips.

# Capricorn (December 22–January 19)

For all the Capricorns out there, you possess one of the most balanced and powerful signs of the zodiac. You can stay focused and organized in any situation. Your consistent behavior means you can carve a unique path to success through dedication, intelligence, and perseverance. As a hardworking Earth sign, you also appreciate creature comforts, making you an excellent provider for yourself and those close to you. Whether it's staying ahead of your personal goals or building relationships with others, Capricorn will surely bring out the best in any situation.

### A. Glyph and Symbol

The glyph of Capricorn is a sea goat, representing the sign's ability to stay afloat in any situation and its ability to adapt. Its symbol is the same.

### B. Keywords

Consistent, Dedicated, Intelligent, and Perseverance.

### C. Element

Capricorn is an Earth sign which symbolizes their practicality and groundedness. It is associated with material comfort, stability, and reliability.

### D. Modality

Capricorn is a Cardinal sign, which means that the sign is focused on initiating projects, leading others, and taking action. They are great at setting goals, taking advantage of opportunities, and getting things done.

### E. Planet

The ruling planet of Capricorn is Saturn, and its influence can be seen in the sign's discipline, focus, and ambition.

### F. Polarity

Capricorn is a Negative sign, meaning they are more focused on internal sources of power than external ones.

### G. Correspondences

- Color: Brown
- Metal: Lead
- Stone: Onyx
- Body Part: The Knees.

# Aquarius (January 20–February 18)

The Aquarius zodiac sign is a unique and interesting one in many ways. Represented by a water bearer, these individuals often possess visionary qualities that could be seen as ahead of their time. They bring a refreshing perspective to the world and tend to think differently than others in various situations. Those born under this sign typically have strong values and come off as quite independent, which gives them a strong aura of resilience. Because of their eccentric nature, Aquarius individuals are fearless problem-solvers known for being outstandingly creative. They are often intuitive and enjoy diving deep into the depths of complex conversations or thoughts. All in all, it's fair to say that having an Aquarius friend or member of your family can make life much more interesting.

### A. Glyph and Symbol

Aquarius's glyph represents water, symbolizing the sign's ability to think deeply and unconventionally. Its symbol is the water bearer, which represents its willingness to offer something unique and valuable.

### B. Keywords

Visionary, Independent, Resourceful, Creative.

### C. Element

Aquarius is an Air sign which symbolizes the sign's inspiration, intellectualism, and originality. It is associated with communication, imagination, and freedom.

### D. Modality

Aquarius is a fixed sign that focuses on maintaining and sustaining projects instead of just initiating them. They are great at staying consistent with their plans and following through with their goals.

### E. Planet

The ruling planet of Aquarius is Uranus. Its influence can be seen in the sign's passion for progress and innovation.

### F. Polarity

Aquarius is a Positive sign, meaning they are more focused on external sources of power than internal ones.

### G. Correspondences

- Color: Electric Blue
- Metal: Uranium
- Stone: Amethyst
- Body Part: The Ankles.

# Pisces (February 19–March 20)

Pisces is one of the most mysterious and compassionate zodiac signs. People born under this sign are always interested in helping, understanding, and supporting others in need. They have a profound ability to see the beauty in everyone else while also connecting with and understanding their own emotions. They are attentive listeners and great problem-solvers who always think outside the box to solve issues. What makes them unique is their ability to empathize deeply with someone and help them without judging or overwhelming them. Pisces will use its creativity and intuition to bring positivity into your life and help you overcome difficult times. Ultimately, Pisces is an old soul living in a modern world, a true beacon of hope for those around them.

### A. Glyph and Symbol

The glyph of Pisces is a representation of two fishes, symbolizing the duality between emotions and reality. Its symbol is two fish tied together, representing the sign's ability to be in tune with themselves and others.

### B. Keywords

Compassionate, Understanding, Empathetic, and Creative.

### C. Element

Pisces is a Water sign which symbolizes the sign's deep emotions and intuition. It is associated with understanding, spiritualism, and sensitivity.

### D. Modality

Pisces is a Mutable sign which means that the sign is well-suited for adapting to change and being flexible in different situations. They are great at trying new things and taking risks when needed.

### E. Planet

The ruling planet of Pisces is Neptune, and its influence can be seen in the sign's dreamy outlook on life.

### F. Polarity

Pisces is a Negative sign, meaning they are more focused on internal sources of power than external ones.

### G. Correspondences

- Color: Sea-Green
- Metal: Platinum
- Stone: Aquamarine
- Body Part: The Feet

Just like each individual, every zodiac sign has aspects that make it unique and special. What's amazing about astrology is the way all the signs are connected. Something true for one sign might also hold true for another, even though the behavior of each sign can vary greatly. It's almost like astrology provides a secret language with which you can better understand yourself and those around you. Knowing how different zodiac signs interact with one another not only helps you to appreciate people better, but it encourages compassion and understanding as well. Whether you believe in astrology or not, it offers an interesting lens through which to view human nature and relationships.

The wheel of zodiac signs is a great way to learn about the twelve-sign zodiac system. It reminds us of how deeply we're connected and how energy travels through the various signs. We can see each sign's unique contribution, such as Aries being a blazing fire sign, Libra balancing the scales with justice, Scorpio digging deep into secrets, and Pisces providing a soothing water element. Not only does it help you to better understand yourself, your strengths, and your weaknesses, but it also helps you comprehend those around you. By looking at the powerful connections between the zodiacs, you can gain valuable insight into your relationships and create more harmonious connections in life.

Take the time to learn more about each sign so you can gain a better understanding of astrology and how it affects you. Studying the zodiac signs is an interesting and enlightening exercise that will help you determine how to best use your energies in life!

# Chapter 5: Sun, Moon, and Rising Signs

Your zodiac sign represents certain traits and characteristics based on when you were born. This additional layer can bring even more insight into your personality. The sun sign details the basics of who you are, such as how you interact with the world around you. On the other hand, moon signs exemplify how your personality and values are formed by past events and experiences. Meanwhile, rising signs indicate your potential hidden talents and qualities, representing an innate functional state which is not influenced by your past. Knowing these can help you better understand yourself so you can live life more fully.

Each zodiac sign manifests differently as sun, moon, rising and descendant sign. [18]

This chapter will discuss the role of each sign, as well as insights gained from each. It will also go through each of the 12 zodiac signs and explain how they manifest as sun, moon, rising, and descendant signs. From this, you should better understand your true self and the immense potential that lies within you. It is your job to unlock and use that potential to the fullest. While this can be difficult, the journey is well worth it.

# Sun Signs

Have you ever wondered what astrological sign matches your personality? Sun signs are an interesting way to learn more about yourself and the people around you. They reveal a great deal about your character traits, from your best qualities to that one annoying habit you can't seem to shake. Knowing your sun sign also gives you an appreciation for how much we have in common with those born under the same sign, which is great food for thought. Whether you believe in it or not, exploring your sun sign can be quite beneficial! It's worth learning more and seeing how accurate they can be.

### Role in Astrology

Sun Signs are an essential part of astrology, providing insight into the unique nature of each sign. People often ask how the position of the stars or planets affects their lives and personalities, and the answer is that it is all determined by astrological signs. They determine a person's zodiac sign, which reveals their tendencies, strengths, and weaknesses. Sun signs are mainly concerned with one's character traits and inner self instead of external events like job opportunities or relationships. Ultimately, looking at someone's sun sign can be a great way to learn more about who they are.

### Insights Provided

One of the most enlightening insights that studying sun signs can provide is understanding your behavior, tendencies, and fate. Knowledge of the twelve zodiac signs allows you to gain a perspective on yourself and others. You can hear countless stories about others, learn how they approach life, and relate to their loved ones to broaden your understanding even more. Sun sign astrology deepens your connection with others by providing invaluable life insights. It can also help you make predictions by bringing structure and direction to where you are headed by symbolically interpreting timing using celestial movements. Learning about individual characteristics associated with each of the astrological signs will provide further clarity about what patterns may arise next for you in your journey.

# Moon Signs

Understanding what your moon sign is can give you greater insight into yourself, as it suggests how you react to your emotions and provides cues to how you deal with stress. It gives information about your inner life, clues about how well you manage personal relationships, giving an idea of who you are underneath the surface. In short, learning your moon sign helps you better grasp yourself and the relationships around you. With some investigation, knowledge, and practice, one can use the moon sign to develop a confident sense of self.

### Role in Astrology

When it comes to astrology, moon signs can be incredibly enlightening. Moon signs can provide insight into your emotional makeup, helping you better understand how emotions influence your reactions and decisions. Whether you are familiar with the basics of astrology or have just discovered it for the first time, recognizing what your moon sign says about you will lead to more self-awareness and greater fulfillment. Each zodiac sign has its unique traits when it comes to emotions. With a deeper understanding of these traits, one can unlock new levels of self-knowledge that are truly powerful and transformative.

### Insights Provided

It's easy to get caught up in the hustle and bustle of daily life, so taking a few moments to learn about your moon sign can give you clarity on how to approach each day. Knowing your moon sign enables you to better understand yourself and the motivations that drive you. It also builds stronger relationships with those around you by helping you recognize what drives their behavior. In addition, understanding your moon sign brings insight into the types of decisions that may bring positive outcomes or ones that will be difficult to recover from. All this knowledge can add up to a more meaningful and purposeful life if taken seriously and correctly used.

People often focus on sun signs, the day and month of your birth, but there's so much more than astrology has to offer. When you look into the placement of your moon sign in astrological houses, you can see what influences you emotionally and spiritually. Knowing this will help you find balance and inner peace in your life. The insight that moon signs can bring about one's emotions, habits, behaviors, and tendencies is invaluable, enabling us to learn our true purpose in life more deeply.

# Rising Signs

Learning about your Rising Sign can be an eye-opening experience. Your Rising Sign is the sign of the zodiac associated with the degree of the eastern horizon at the time of your birth. Based on your location and time zone, it takes into account the precise position of the sun on Earth. Looking up your Rising Sign can give you an incredibly unique insight into what kind of person you are and why you have certain personality traits or perspectives that set you apart from others. Knowing more about your Rising Sign is a great way to understand yourself better and be proud of who you are!

### Role in Astrology

In astrology, the rising sign has a crucial role to play. Often referred to as your "ascendant," it is the sign that was rising on the horizon at the exact moment of your birth and can tell you a lot about your external personality traits and how you present yourself to others. Rising signs explain why two people with similar sun signs may have drastically different personalities. Someone's rising sign truly makes them unique! The fact that all of this is determined by just one moment in time speaks to the incredible complexity and beauty of astrology.

### Insights Provided

The rising sign, also known as the ascendant, provides a deeper level of self-knowledge and understanding. It is as crucial to an individual's birth chart as the Sun, Moon, and other planets. Your rising sign directly impacts how you relate to the world around you, your outlook on life, and your relationship with others. Knowing more about it can help provide insights into why certain complications or issues arise in areas such as relationships and career paths. With the right interpretation, it can reveal things like why we respond emotionally in a certain way or even why we feel something is lacking in a relationship. Seeking professional advice or taking some time to explore a birth chart can enable us to use our rising signs to gain greater clarity on ourselves and life's journey.

# Descendants

Astrology is an ancient tradition with numerous applications and interpretations which can help you to better understand the world. One such area of study, particularly interesting in modern times, is the study of the Descendant in astrology. The descendant shows how you relate to and interact with those around you, including family, friends, and peers. It often reveals your hidden personality traits as well as how you show up in relationships of all kinds. Knowing these components of who you are can be extremely helpful for a person's journey in this life. Understanding the descendant and what it symbolizes can be tricky, but with a bit of research and exploration of astrology tools like charts or zodiac symbols, you, too, can learn more about yourself.

### Role In Astrology

Many people have heard of a birth chart in astrology and know that it is divided into 12 sections, each representing an area of life. However, few know what the "Descendant" represents. The Descendant is the sign on the 7th house cusp and often symbolizes your relationships with others, both platonic and romantic. It can show unique aspects of your character, which may be found through intimate relationships or partnerships, along with how you go about creating those connections. People who are knowledgeable in astrology believe the Descendant plays a significant role in understanding yourself and even predicting your future.

### Insights Provided

Astrology has many fascinating topics that can offer amazing insights into ourselves and our futures. One of these is the concept of a descendant, which traditionally marks the seventh house in an astrological chart. The descendant represents relationships in your life and how you operate within them and are perceived by others. It offers very valuable insights into yourself, such as how you handle intimacy, collaborations, and your one-on-one connections.

Additionally, it influences how we deal with public perceptions of us and allows us to be aware of potential issues. Knowing about your descendant within astrology can offer a lot of insight into your relationships and why you attract specific people or situations in your life. Understanding yourself better can lead to stronger and more fulfilling connections with those around you. So, get out there and learn about yours!

# Zodiac Signs Revisited

It's time to revisit your beloved zodiac sign and explore what else can tell you about yourself! The traditional sun sign, determined by the month and date of your birthday, only gives a basic overview of someone's personality. A whole new layer of complexity is revealed when you look at people's birth charts based on the moon sign and rising sign. The moon sign symbolizes your innermost feelings and emotions, while the rising sign reveals how others experience you, and this combination creates a unique portrait of each individual. With an ever-changing universe around you impacting your daily life, taking into account your three signs together can help shed some light on what makes you tick.

# Aries

Aries is a bold, passionate, and energetic sign that can bring an extra spark to any conversation, project, or situation.

### As a Sun Sign

With Aries as your sun sign, you are full of courage and ambition, making you determined to get things done.

### As a Moon Sign

Your moon sign reflects your emotions and the inner person you are. Aries moons are not afraid to express their moods, feel at ease, and be honest about life's ups and downs.

### As a Rising Sign

Your rising sign is the public face you present to the world, which for Aries, might be represented by strength and determination. There's no stopping an Aries once they set their sights on something!

### As A Descendant

Your Descendant reveals how you handle relationships as an Aries, and with this sign can come boldness when it comes to romantic pursuits. They tend to be fiercely loyal and passionate when it comes to their relationships. This can sometimes come off as intense, but they are ultimately looking to settle down with someone they truly love and trust.

# Taurus

Taurus is a steady, reliable sign that often prefers to take it slow and steady.

### As A Sun Sign

People with Taurus as their sun sign are often down-to-earth and have a strong sense of self-worth. They know what they need and aren't afraid to take what's theirs.

### As a Moon Sign

Taurus moons feel strongly about their beliefs, rarely taking them lightly and often challenging those around them.

### As a Rising Sign

A Taurian rising sign usually tells the world that this person is reliable and loyal, something that tends to attract admirers.

### As a Descendant

Someone with Taurus as their descendant shows the world their need to be respected and appreciated. They are often looking for the same kind of steady love and support in their relationships as they give, rarely settling for anything less.

# Gemini

Gemini is a dualistic sign that loves to explore the world around them.

### As a Sun Sign

Geminis are inquisitive by nature, often having a passion for knowledge and the pursuit of adventure.

### As a Moon Sign

Gemini moons are often quite sensitive and can be hard on themselves, making it difficult to open up to others.

### As a Rising Sign

A Gemini rising sign usually indicates adaptability to new situations and people, making it easy for them to fit in quickly.

### As a Descendant

Geminis with a descendant sign are often looking for someone to help bring their ideas and dreams to life. They can be fiercely passionate in their relationships and are always looking for something to explore and new heights to reach.

# Cancer

Cancer is a nurturing sign that loves to take care of their loved ones.

### As a Sun Sign

People with Cancer as their sun sign are often quite compassionate and caring, putting the needs of others first.

### As a Moon Sign

Cancer moons are deeply emotional and can often be overwhelmed by their feelings.

### As a Rising Sign

A Cancerian rising sign shows others that this person is kind and gentle, often looking out for the needs of those around them.

### As a Descendant

Cancerians with a descendant sign typically show the world how much they need to feel deeply connected and loved in their relationships. They are often looking for someone who can share an emotional bond with them, someone who can understand their feelings and appreciate them for who they are.

# Leo

Leo is an energetic sign that loves to be the center of attention.

### As a Sun Sign

People with Leo as their sun sign are often confident and have a flare for being the center of attention.

### As a Moon Sign

Leo moons can be quite expressive and often need to express themselves artistically.

### As a Rising Sign

A Leonian rising sign might show others that this person is passionate and ambitious, often looking to make an impact on the world around them.

### As a Descendant

Leos with a descendant sign are often looking for someone who can appreciate their boldness and enthusiasm. They need to be with someone who encourages them to keep striving forward while also providing them with the support and security they need to feel comfortable.

# Virgo

Virgo is a practical sign that loves to help others.

### As a Sun Sign

People with Virgo as their sun sign are often quite detail-oriented and strive for perfection.

### As a Moon Sign

Virgo moons are analytical by nature and can often be hard on themselves, looking for ways to improve and grow.

### As a Rising Sign

A Virgo rising sign usually shows that this person is organized and dependable, often taking on the role of helping others.

### As a Descendant

Virgos with a descendant sign are often looking for someone who can help them find balance and stability in their relationships. They need to be with someone who is there for them when they need it while also giving them the freedom to grow and explore.

# Libra

Libra is a harmonious sign that loves beauty and justice.

### As a Sun Sign

People with Libra as their sun sign are often quite diplomatic and strive to keep the peace.

### As a Moon Sign

Libra moons are often quite idealistic, looking for ways to bring balance and harmony into the world.

### As a Rising Sign

A Libra rising sign usually indicates that this person is sociable and graceful, often looking to bring people together.

### As a Descendant

Librans with a descendant sign typically need someone who can appreciate their big-picture thinking and help them stay grounded. They need to be with someone who is there for them when they need it while also giving them the freedom to express themselves.

# Scorpio

Scorpio is an intense sign that loves to explore the depths of the unknown.

### As a Sun Sign

People with Scorpio as their sun sign are often quite passionate and have a strong drive for transformation.

### As a Moon Sign

Scorpio moons can be quite secretive and often need to explore their emotions to better understand themselves.

### As a Rising Sign

A Scorpio rising sign usually indicates that this person is a mystery to outsiders, often looking to uncover the secrets of the world.

### As a Descendant

Scorpios with a descendant sign are often looking for someone who can bring out their softer side while also understanding and respecting their need for privacy. They need to be with someone who can appreciate their intensity and passion while also giving them the space to explore their own emotions.

# Sagittarius

Sagittarius is a philosophical sign that loves to explore the world.

### As A Sun Sign

People with Sagittarius as their sun sign are often quite adventurous and seek out new experiences.

### As A Moon Sign

Sagittarius moons are often quite optimistic and strive to bring joy and optimism into the world.

### As a Rising Sign

A Sagittarian rising sign usually shows that this person is fun-loving and enthusiastic, often looking to expand their horizons.

### As a Descendant

Sagittarians with a descendant sign often need someone who can encourage them to stay focused and grounded while also appreciating their love of learning and exploration. They need to be with someone who can bring balance and stability into their lives while also giving them the freedom to explore new ideas.

# Capricorn

Capricorn is an ambitious sign that loves to take on new challenges.

### As a Sun Sign

People with Capricorn as their sun sign are often quite goal-oriented and strive to achieve success.

### As a Moon Sign

Capricorn moons can be quite serious and often need to find ways to connect with others to better understand themselves.

### As a Rising Sign

A Capricornian rising sign usually indicates that this person is determined and practical, often looking to build something tangible.

### As a Descendant

Capricorns with a descendant sign are often looking for someone who can bring out their softer side and help them relax and unwind. They need to be with someone who can provide guidance and support while also giving them the freedom to pursue their goals.

# Aquarius

Aquarius is a curious sign that loves to explore the unknown.

### As a Sun Sign

People with Aquarius as their sun sign are often quite progressive and strive to bring about positive change.

### As a Moon Sign

Aquarius moons can be quite rebellious and often need to express their individuality to better understand themselves.

### As a Rising Sign

An Aquarian rising sign usually indicates that this person is independent and progressive, often looking to push the boundaries of convention.

### As a Descendant

Aquarians with a descendant sign are often looking for someone who can bring out their softer side and help them feel secure. They need to be with someone who can appreciate their uniqueness and individuality while also giving them the space to explore their ideas.

# Pisces

Pisces is a compassionate sign that loves to help others.

### As a Sun Sign

People with Pisces as their sun sign are often quite dreamy and strive to bring peace and balance into the world.

### As a Moon Sign

Pisces moons can be quite sensitive and often need to express their emotions to better understand themselves.

### As a Rising Sign

A Pisces rising sign usually indicates that this person is gentle and kind-hearted, often looking to nurture the people around them.

### As a Descendant

Pisces with a descendant sign are often looking for someone who can bring out their strength and confidence. They need to be with someone who can encourage them to take risks and be assertive while also giving them the space to explore their own emotions.

Overall, each zodiac sign can manifest in different ways depending on its placement in the birth chart, so it's crucial to consider all of these factors when interpreting a person's astrological chart. By gaining a deeper understanding of the sun, moon, rising sign, and descendant in an individual's birth chart, you can gain insight into the person's character, qualities, and behaviors. Whether you are looking for guidance in your own life or want to better understand the people around you, delving into the world of astrology can be a great way to gain insight and clarity.

The knowledge in this chapter can provide a greater depth of understanding about how they communicate with others, their values and beliefs, their emotional needs and wants, as well as how they manifest their highest potential. With this knowledge increasing our awareness of these cosmic influences on each individual uniquely, we can develop more meaningful connections with those around us by appreciating the various intricacies that make up the people in our lives.

# Chapter 6: The Houses I. Ego, Resources, and the Mind

Astrology is a fascinating study of the effects that planets, stars, and other celestial bodies have on physical and psychological life. One of its key components, which is sometimes overlooked, is the birth chart houses. Each house has an individual, symbolic meaning that speaks to different aspects of life, such as home, family, and relationships. These houses serve as a guideline for understanding and interpreting astrological information in a more personalized way. These

Astrological houses.[14]

insights can be conveniently combined with other astrological interpretations to get a full scope of how stars influence your life on Earth.

This chapter will explore the individual houses of the birth chart. We will explore each house thoroughly by looking at cusps, keywords, themes, and the effects of different planets and zodiac signs in each house. Understanding each house gives you a better insight into how the stars influence your life on Earth. With this knowledge, each person can better understand their natural inclinations and motivators, using the planets' placement at their birth time.

## Houses in Astrology

Astrology is a fascinating subject, full of depth and complexity. Did you know that it uses the concept of twelve houses to represent different aspects of life? These houses are used when interpreting an astrological chart, and each one speaks to a particular area, such as home, money, friends, career, and more. It's incredibly interesting how all of these specific areas of life can be characterized by an ancient symbolic system. Even if you're not an astrology enthusiast yourself, it's worth taking the time to appreciate how detailed and insightful this practice can be.

The 12 houses.

# House Cusps

Have you ever noticed similarities between people with the same astrology sign? It turns out there is more to interpreting your birth chart than just knowing your sun sign! The concept of house cusps in astrology adds another layer to create a more comprehensive picture of who you are and how the universe shapes you. House cusps are the points that divide your natal chart into 12 sections (or houses); each represents certain aspects of your personality. By studying where powerful planets like Jupiter and Saturn fall about the house cusps, you can gain valuable insights into how your energy plays off against different parts of life, helping you to understand more about yourself and others.

### Theme

The theme of the houses is dependent on the house in question. The first house, for example, is known as the "house of ego" and speaks to themes like self-expression, identity, and early life experiences. The second house is known as the "house of resources" and speaks to themes like money, possessions, and material security. The third house, meanwhile, is known as the "house of mind" and speaks to themes like communication, education, and siblings. In general, each house speaks to a particular part of life, with the zodiac sign ruling that house plays a major role in how it is interpreted.

### Planet/Sign Analysis

The zodiac sign ruling each house plays a major role in how it is interpreted. For example, if your birth chart has Aries ruling the first house, you can expect to have a strong sense of courage and independence in your life. If Scorpio rules the eighth house, then you can expect to have keen insights into the depths of yourself and others. In addition, the planets in each house also play a role in how it is interpreted. Planets like the Sun, which represents our ego identity, can give you an insight into how you express and interact with others in the world. Meanwhile, the Moon, which represents your inner emotions and subconscious desires, can give you an insight into how you relate to yourself on a deeper level.

# The First House: Ego

The first house in astrology symbolizes the ego or how a person presents themselves to the world. This is an important factor in determining a person's fate and destiny throughout life. It's no surprise that those with strong first houses tend to project their confidence and inner will powerfully to make an impact on the world around them. For those with weak first houses, it can pay to put in some extra effort to get yourself out without feeling judged or labeled by others. After all, humans are here for a short time, so make sure you express yourself.

### Ruling Zodiac Sign and Planet

Aries, the first sign of the zodiac, and Mars, the planet of ambition and drive, both gracefully rule the first house. With the combination of the two great forces, this house contains a warrior-like energy that is unparalleled. People guided by this power are formidable forces to be reckoned with who dare to take on life's difficult challenges without retreating or wrapping up in their comfort zone. Those born under Aries and Mars know that no challenge is too great for them to tackle as long as they use their inner strength and determination to reach their goals. There may be times along the way when big obstacles arise, but that fiery energy will not falter until success is obtained.

### House Cusps and Meaning

The house cusp of the first house is known as the Ascendant (also called the Rising sign). It marks the beginning of your journey into the world and provides a clue as to how You'll approach life. The Descendant, meanwhile, marks the end of your journey in the world and gives you insight into how you will leave your mark.

Medium Coeli (MC) and Imum Coeli (IC) are two other important points in the chart which are related to the house cusps. MC represents your public persona, while IC speaks to your private persona. These points can give you insight into how the outside world views you and the inner parts of yourself that remain hidden.

### Main Keywords

The main keywords associated with the first house are ambition, purpose, identity, self-expression, and courage.

### Description of the House's Theme

The first house represents a person's character, personality, and approach to life. It speaks to how you express yourself, your motivations and goals, and how you interact with others. This is the house of ego where you form your identity and project it out into the world. It is also a house of courage and inner will, as it takes guts to stand up for yourself and take risks to make an impact. The first house speaks to the very foundations of your being, and it is important to pay attention to how you present yourself to the world.

### Planet/Sign Analysis

The ruling planet and the sign of the first house play a major role in how it is interpreted. The sign of Aries and planet Mars gives the first house its fiery energy, emphasizing ambition, strength, and a desire to take risks to make an impact. The Sun, meanwhile, is the planet of identity and ego, and it gives you insight into how you express yourself to the world. The Moon also plays an important role as it represents your inner emotions and subconscious desires. It helps you understand your relationship with yourself and how you can nurture it to grow and become the best version of yourself.

Overall, the first house is a powerful tool to explore your identity and how it affects your life journey. It provides insight into how you present yourself to the world and how you can use your inner fire and courage to make an impact. Paying attention to this house can help you to understand yourself better and take control of your destiny.

## The Second House: Resources

The second house of astrology is known as the house of resources, and it deals with money, possessions, self-confidence, and material security. It clarifies how you utilize your resources for growth and stability. This house affects profit through work, inheritance, taxes, investments, the increased value of assets, and pay raises. Your concern for tangible valuables such as physical objects, wealth, acquisitions, and comfort items also falls under this section. This house also reflects your capacity to hold on to or let go of the material things in your life with acceptance or resolutions. Astrology can help you to understand how your financial decisions may be influenced by the planets and lead you to form a successful approach to managing resources both materially and psychologically.

### Ruling Zodiac Sign and Planet

The Second House is one of the most interesting places to explore in the celestial sky. This house is ruled by the Zodiac sign of Taurus, along with the planet Venus. It helps you look into how you use money and other resources to ensure your security and where your values come from. Plus, it can provide insights into what type of possessions bring you joy, material or otherwise. Knowing your second house can organize your finances and make sure that you're making wise decisions when it comes to spending and saving; exploring it will expand your cosmic consciousness.

### House Cusps and Meaning

The cusp of the second house is known as the "Cadent," and it speaks to your ability to manage resources, both materially and psychologically. It is associated with the concept of "wealth," and it reflects your capacity to hold on to or let go of material things in your life.

### Main Keywords

The main keywords associated with the second house are resources, money, possessions, self-confidence, and material security.

### Description of the House's Theme

The second house is all about material security, how you use your resources to create wealth, and your capacity to manage money. It represents what you own in the physical world and how you use it to create stability for yourself. This house also speaks to your self-esteem and how you feel about your worth. It reflects the kind of relationship you have with money, possessions, and physical objects and how those relationships can either help or hinder them. By understanding the second house, you can gain insight into how you can use your resources to create the kind of life you want for yourself.

### Planet/Sign Analysis

Taurus and Venus are the rulers of the second house, and their influence can be seen in how we handle our resources. Taurus is a sign of stability and practicality, encouraging you to take a practical approach to money and possessions. Venus is the planet of values, and it helps you to understand what you value in life and how you can use your resources to create stability. When these two planets are combined, they give you the ability to manage your resources practically and meaningfully.

Overall, the second house of astrology can be a powerful tool for understanding your relationship with money and possessions. It provides insight into how you can use your resources to create the kind of life you desire and build the stability you need for long-term success. By paying attention to this house, you can better understand your finances and how you can use them to create the kind of life you want.

# The Third House: The Mind

The third house of astrology is a fascinating realm of study. Ruling the realm of information and the mind can be seen as a gateway to understanding how you interact with the world around you. It looks at the things that affect your decisions and actions, from communication to education to which theories you hold true. As humans, you must examine every part of your life to evolve and grow. Examining the third house is one way to do just that. With deeper knowledge comes a greater connection to yourself, and unlocking the secrets of this mysterious place can lead you to major discoveries about yourself and your world.

### Ruling Zodiac Sign and Planet

The third house, also known as the house of the mind, is ruled by the zodiac sign Gemini and the planet Mercury. Ruled by Gemini, this house is related to communication, mental connections between people, thoughts, ideas, and beliefs you hold to be true. Think about it, Gemini is always on the go, socializing and chatting as it loves exchanging ideas! Meanwhile, Mercury calls for clear thinking. It pertains to your ability to process information quickly and apply intelligence reliably. Overall, this house deals with how you make sense of information mentally and verbally.

### House Cusps and Meaning

The cusp of the third house, known as the "Succedent," is all about information, how you take it in, and how you process it. It represents the way you learn, think, and express your thoughts.

### Main Keywords

The main keywords associated with the third house are communication, education, networking, learning, and analysis.

### Description of the House's Theme

The third house is the realm of communication, intellectual pursuits, and learning. Here, you can explore your thought processes, how you take in information, and how you express yourself to the world. It is a house of education, understanding how you use your knowledge to make sense of the world around you and how you interact with others. It looks at how you learn and use your knowledge to grow. It also speaks to your ability to connect with others, understand their perspectives, and build meaningful relationships.

**Planet/Sign Analysis**

Gemini and Mercury are the rulers of the third house, and their influence can be seen in how we think and communicate. Gemini is a sign of intelligence and communication, encouraging you to explore new ideas and express yourself without fear. Mercury is the planet of logic and reason, helping you make sense of the world around you and understand different perspectives. When these two planets are combined, they give you the tools to think critically and communicate ideas effectively.

Overall, the third house of astrology is a powerful tool for understanding how you think, communicate, and learn. It provides insight into your intellectual pursuits and the way you take in information from the world around you. By examining this house, you can better understand your thought process and how it shapes your actions.

Exploring the houses of astrology can be an illuminating experience, providing insight into all areas of life, from behavior patterns to relationships. Looking deeper into each one can give you a better understanding of your personality and the motivation for different choices and experiences. They even advise how you can respond to the challenges and opportunities that come your way.

Looking at the houses of astrology can provide you with invaluable wisdom that might otherwise remain unknown, often giving more satisfying answers than "just follow your gut." With this knowledge, we can gain greater insight into ourselves and how we interact with the world. By exploring the houses of astrology, you can better understand how you move through life and the choices that come your way.

# Chapter 7: The Houses II. Home, Creativity, and Health

Astrology has been around for centuries and fascinates and influences people even today. The concept of houses, composed of 12 divisions, indicates where a celestial body (like the sun or the moon) is positioned relative to your life at a given moment in time. The various astrological houses each represent different areas of your life. Knowing and understanding this information can be incredibly valuable to gain deeper insight into yourself, as it provides an objective look into your past, present, and future circumstances.

This chapter will focus on the fourth, fifth, and sixth astrological houses. It will dive into each of these houses to explore them thoroughly. It will also look at the ruling zodiac sign and planet, house cusps and their meanings, the main keywords that describe them, a description of each house's theme, and a brief analysis of the effects and lessons of each planet and zodiac sign in that house. With this knowledge, you can work through any difficulties or issues that life throws at you more effectively.

## The Fourth House: The Home

The fourth astrological house is often thought of as where the soul's most intimate home lies. Rich with symbolism and cultural significance, studying this house has the potential to offer powerful insights into the individual and the role their home plays in their life. Many look to this house to uncover what they prioritize and value, with various aspects within it, across boundaries, communication, siblings, and transportation, helping people work out not only how these things have impacted them personally but how they can use them going forward to achieve their goals.

From an astrological viewpoint, the concept of "home" spans far beyond the physical aspects of having a roof over your head and the security it affords you. Home is so much more than just tangible property. It's about how you attach yourself to space, people, and places and energetically connect in ways that shape how you exist on a grand scale. Moving from this perspective allows you to get a fuller understanding of home as part of your unique map on this Earth.

With some reflection and exploration, you can see how each area has its own set of archetypes, traditions, environmental conditions, and world view that greatly shapes your experience in life. Understanding these dynamics can add tremendous richness to the idea of home and provide even deeper insight into who you are as an individual.

### Ruling Zodiac Sign and Planet

Gemini and its ruling planet, Mercury, are an interesting combination. When these two heavenly bodies work together, they can bring a wide variety of influences to the fourth house. Outgoing Gemini energy supplies the inquisitiveness for wanting to learn and explore, while Mercury provides the communication skills, clear thinking, and mental agility necessary for information gathering. As such, expect plenty of intellectual stimulation regarding all matters related to this house.

### House Cusps and Their Meaning

The cusp of the fourth house is usually associated with the sign of Gemini, and it is often referred to as the "Gemini Gate." This cusp marks a pivotal point in life's journey, as it signifies the beginning of self-expression and exploration. The cusp of Gemini is a starting point for any new idea, concept, or belief system. It's the point at which you can start applying your knowledge and understanding of the world around you to find your place.

### Main Keywords

The main keywords for the fourth astrological house are communication, ideas, information, exploration, travel, and siblings. The fourth astrological house is all about communicating, expanding your intellectual horizons, connecting with others, and exploring new places. It's a great opportunity to expand your knowledge and understanding of the world around us. The main keywords associated with this house are all potential growth areas for anyone who chooses to pay attention to them. Whether it means exchanging stories with a sibling or embarking on a journey far from home, this house encourages you to explore the world around you to make the most of your life.

### Description of the House's Theme

The fourth house is all about communication and the exchange of ideas. It is also associated with travel and exploration, representing the desire to venture into the world and gain knowledge. The fourth house has a strong connection to siblings, as it is the house of early childhood and family development. This house is a place of growth and learning where individuals can expand their minds and discover new perspectives.

### Planet/Sign Analysis

Mercury has a strong influence over the fourth house, as it is associated with communication and understanding. With its powers of eloquence, quick wit, and mental agility, Mercury can help an individual gain a greater understanding of the world around them. This is further enhanced when its influence is combined with that of Gemini, the sign associated with this house. Gemini energy is curious and eager to explore, making it a perfect match for Mercury's more intellectual and analytical side. These two forces can create a powerful combination that leads to greater personal growth and understanding.

The sign Gemini is also associated with siblings and this house, as it reflects the connection between two people. This relationship can be a source of great joy, but it can also be a source of conflict. Gemini energy encourages open dialogue and understanding, which can help to resolve any issues that arise. It is also a sign of exploration and learning, which can lead to discoveries and insights. Finally, Gemini can also be a great source of encouragement and support as it encourages individuals to reach their full potential.

Overall, the fourth house is about communication, exploration, and a better understanding of oneself and the world around them. It is a place of growth and learning where individuals can find new perspectives and gain greater insight into their own identities. Through its connection to the planet Mercury and the sign Gemini, this house can provide an abundance of mental stimulation and exploration that leads to personal growth.

# The Fifth House: Creativity

The fifth house of Astrology is a fascinating area of study that explores the creative energies within us. This house focuses on creative areas like hobbies, artistic expression, and even hospitality. It's the part within you that allows you to be creative and try new things. It's also associated with your innermost emotions and feelings of home and family, which can greatly influence your creative endeavors. Exploring this house can lead to discovering hidden talents and a newfound appreciation for your innate creativity.

By recognizing the fifth house in astrology, you can answer questions like "what drives me? What abilities do I possess? How do I recreate my life and discover who I truly am?" This knowledge allows for a greater understanding of yourself and your relationships with others. So why not leap and dive into this mystical world of insight? You may be surprised at the power of your imagination when coupled with cosmic wisdom.

### Ruling Zodiac Sign and Planet

The fifth house is ruled by the zodiac sign of Cancer and the planet Moon. The influence of these two planets gives this house an emotionally charged energy, as the Moon governs our innermost feelings and emotions. Cancer energy is also strongly associated with home, comfort, and security, providing a safe and nurturing environment for creativity to flourish. This combination of energies allows for a profound connection with the inner self and encourages individuals to explore their full potential.

### House Cusps and Meaning

The fifth house is represented by the cusps of Imum Coeli and Medium Coeli. Imum Coeli, Latin for "the lowest of the heavens," represents the bottom tier of the zodiac and is associated with home, family, and inner feelings. This cusp is a gateway to the soul and encourages individuals to explore their spiritual side. On the other hand, Medium Coeli, Latin for "the middle of the heavens," is associated with intellectual pursuits and higher education. This cusp allows for exploration into the world of knowledge and encourages individuals to broaden their horizons.

### Main Keywords

The main keywords for the fifth house are creativity, home, emotions, family, inner feelings, exploration, and spirituality. It's certainly a place of comfort and solace, but it is capable of so much more. Every part of this house holds something special, from the creativity it brings out in people to its ability to nurture family life and emotions. It helps one explore the depths of their inner feelings through its spiritual guidance, creating a space where one can feel secure and at home with themselves. With all these beautiful aspects, it's no wonder why many people who come into contact with the fifth house feel so connected.

### Description of House Theme

The fifth house in astrology is about discovering the creative potential within us. It encourages individuals to explore their innermost emotions and life's possibilities. This house is also associated with home and family, which can serve as a strong source of guidance and support to those who seek it. This house's energies allow you to express your feelings and discover a newfound appreciation for yourself.

### Planet/Sign Analysis

The energy of the Moon and Cancer gives the fifth house a strong emotional charge. The Moon, associated with feminine energy, is all about connecting to your innermost feelings and emotions. Conversely, cancer is associated with home and family life, which can give you a greater sense of security and stability. Together, these energies can help individuals to explore their creative potential in a safe and nurturing environment. With the Moon's influence, you can tap into your innermost desires and express yourself meaningfully. With the energy of Cancer, you can find comfort and security in your family life, allowing you to explore your creative talents with a greater sense of ease.

The fifth house in astrology encourages individuals to explore their inner world and tap into their true potential. By recognizing the importance of home and family, you can discover a newfound appreciation for your creative talents and better understand yourself and your relationships with others. With the energy of Cancer and the Moon, you can explore your innermost feelings in a safe and nurturing environment and tap into your creative potential. By exploring the fifth house in astrology, you can gain greater insight into yourself and be more in tune with your emotions. This can ultimately help you find your creative voice and unlock your potential.

# The Sixth House: Health

The sixth house of astrology, the House of Health, indicates how healthy and strong we are in our bodies. This house is thought to be connected to our overall physical state as well as our vitality. It also plays a role in detailing where your health weaknesses may lie. To evaluate your health from an astrological point of view, you'll need to take a look at this house and observe how the different planets are placed within it. This will help you figure out what health challenges might be present in your life and offer advice on ways to stay healthy and alert. Keep in mind that staying physically active, eating right, and getting enough sleep can go a long way in helping you remain healthy overall.

## Ruling Zodiac Sign and Planet

The sixth house, ruled by Leo and the Sun, is an area of your chart that inherently focuses on enjoyment. This can be anything from creative hobbies to deep-seated passions, allowing you to take a break from life's struggles and just have fun. Leo's influence suggests here it's all about celebrating the best bits of yourself, your confident persona, and the brave new ideas that help shape who you are. It's a place to feel truly alive, bask in your light, and show yourself some love. With the Sun as ruler of this part of your journey, make sure you take time out of every day to take pleasure in life.

## Main Keywords

While it may not be the most-talked-about house, this house has some interesting things to offer. It's connected to health, vitality, energy, and physical well-being. So, if you're feeling out of sorts or need to hit the reset button on your own wellness goals, this could be a great spot to check out in your astrological chart. It also brings pleasure, joy, creativity, leisure activities (think yoga and painting classes), and general happiness. So, remember that if you're looking for some enthusiasm and satisfaction, the sixth house just might be the answer!

## Description of the House's Theme

The sixth house in astrology is associated with overall health and well-being. It speaks to the vitality that you have within yourself, as well as your physical strength. This house can also reveal areas of weakness within your health and how to address these issues. Additionally, it speaks to the pleasure and joy you experience through creative hobbies, passions, and leisure activities. The sixth house is a place to celebrate the best parts of yourself, bask in your light, and be nurturing toward yourself. It's also a place to explore new ideas and activities that help shape your identity.

**Planet/Sign Analysis**

The Sun, the ruler of this house, is associated with creativity and joy. It allows you to explore your creative side and take pleasure in life. With the Sun in this house, you can feel energized and alive when expressing yourself through your passions and hobbies. Leo is also associated with this house, which brings a sense of confidence and boldness. It encourages you to be your true self and enjoy being unique. With this sign, you can feel fearless in your pursuits and find the courage to take risks. The Moon is associated with nurturing and caring for yourself, which is key to health and well-being. This planet helps you to take a closer look at your emotions, allowing you to tap into your needs and prioritize yourself.

Overall, the sixth house in astrology helps you gain insight into your physical health and overall sense of joy and pleasure. It encourages you to explore your passions, take risks, and be confident. By tapping into the energies of this house, you can learn to prioritize your health and well-being and find joy in life's little pleasures.

The fourth house in astrology is a powerful space that speaks about your home, family, and daily routines. By taking a closer look at this house, you can gain insight into how you interact with your environment and the people around you. You can also gain insight into your overall sense of joy and pleasure, allowing you to take time out of life's struggles and have fun.

The fifth house in astrology is an equally powerful space connected to your creativity, passions, and leisure activities. By tapping into this house's energies, you can learn to prioritize your health and well-being, take risks, and find joy in life's little pleasures. Ultimately, the sixth house reminds you to take time out of your day for your health and well-being, as well as for creative pursuits and leisure activities. By exploring this house, you can better understand yourself and how you are connected to the world around you.

# Chapter 8: The Houses III. Relationships, Growth, and Travel

The astrological houses are an essential part of any astrological study. Through these twelve houses, you gain insight into yourself and your surroundings. Each house has its unique meaning, characterized by the planetary ruler it is associated with. Studying the houses can allow you to better understand both the cosmic energies at work within your life and how they affect people close to you. This knowledge can provide deeper insight into relationships, life paths, goals, and more. The astrological houses make it possible to understand yourself at a whole new level.

This chapter will dive into the zodiac's seventh, eighth, and ninth houses and explain their meanings in detail. It will start by exploring the seventh house, which is all about relationships. It will then move on to the eighth house, which focuses on growth and transformation. Finally, the ninth house, which is all about travel and higher learning, will be discussed. Each house will be analyzed regarding its ruling zodiac sign and planet, house cusps and their meanings, main keywords, a description of the house's theme, and finally, a brief analysis of each planet/sign in the house. By the end, you should better understand astrological houses and how they affect your life.

# The Seventh House: Relationships

The seventh astrological house is all about relationships and covers every type of relationship you can think of. From deep romantic love to lifelong friendships to working partnerships with your colleagues, this house of the zodiac can tell you a lot about your connection with others. It looks at how you come together and combines your strengths and how you handle communication in relationships. You can learn a lot from analyzing the seventh house, allowing you to connect better with the people around you. So why not look up what it reveals about your relationships and discover how to strengthen them?

### Ruling Zodiac Sign and Planet

The seventh house is ruled by Libra and also by Venus. Libra, the sign of balance, harmony, and justice, helps you to understand how to nurture relationships. Venus, the planet of love and beauty, encourages you to seek out relationships that bring peace and joy.

### House Cusps and Their Meaning

The seventh house is cusped by the Descendant and the Medium Coeli (MC). The Descendant marks the beginning of the seventh house, indicating where you are open to new relationships. The Medium Coeli is the highest point in this house, symbolizing the pinnacle of success in a relationship. It also shows what you can learn from your relationships and how you can use them to grow.

### Main Keywords

The seventh astrological house has so much to offer in terms of analyzing interpersonal relationships. The main keywords associated with the seventh astrological house are relationships, partnerships, commitments, compromise, communication, and balance. This house helps you unpack the challenges and celebrations that come with sharing life with another person, whether a love partner, family member – or even a pet.

Here you make commitments, both big and small, and can identify areas where compromise is necessary. To ensure smooth communication and balanced relationships, it is essential to understand how your needs relate to another's to achieve strong dynamic partnerships. The seventh house is where we can begin learning this valuable lesson. The seventh house teaches you that relationships are a two-way street and you should never be afraid to speak up for yourself.

### Description of the House's Theme

The seventh astrological house is where relationships and partnerships take the spotlight. This house focuses on understanding your own needs, as well as those of your partner, on creating a balanced and healthy relationship. It is here that you learn how to compromise with others while also staying true to yourself. This house looks at the dynamics of a relationship, from its beginnings to its inevitable end. It also teaches you that all relationships will have their ups and downs and that it is important to communicate effectively to navigate any issues that come up.

### Planet/Sign Analysis

Libra, the ruler of the seventh house, encourages us to aim for harmony and balance in our relationships. Libra helps you recognize what you need from a partner and what you can bring to the table. Venus, also ruling this house, is the planet of love and beauty. It inspires you to nurture your relationships and make them stronger. Both planets help you to understand how your relationships can benefit from communication, compromise, and mutual understanding. No matter what kind of relationship you are looking to nurture, the seventh house can help you find a way.

By diving deeper into the seventh house, you can gain insight into your relationships and learn how to make them stronger. From understanding the dynamics of a relationship to finding balance, the seventh house is full of knowledge that can help you grow. By exploring this house, you can become better connected with the people you care about and create lasting relationships.

## The Eighth House: Growth

The eighth house in astrology has a mystique all its own. It is associated with transformation and growth, allowing you to go through powerful changes which allow for accelerated personal growth. Additionally, the eighth house rules health, finance, and sex, the latter of which will forever remain shrouded in mystery. It can be uncomfortable thinking about those topics in detail or even at all, but it can be eye-opening when you do so with an open mind. Examining your life through the lens of this mysterious house has tremendous potential to unlock hidden meanings and deepen your understanding of life.

It's related to the idea of transformation and speaks to the depth of your life as you enter into a space that touches upon taboo topics such as sexuality and death. This eighth house is all about getting down to the nitty-gritty details of life and experiencing evolution through challenging times. By facing mortality and embracing sex as a natural part of being human, you can embrace growth in a way that takes you to deeper levels of self-knowledge. Understanding this house opens up a path for you to understand yourself even more!

### Ruling Zodiac Sign and Planet

The eighth house is ruled by Scorpio and Pluto, both of which carry a connotation of mystery and darkness. They can represent confronting and uncomfortable aspects of life that we may prefer to avoid. However, although this house can bring with it some difficult lessons and uncertainties, it also brings powerful growth opportunities. Pluto's transformative energy can be incredibly empowering if we let it. Scorpio encourages you to dig deep into the depths of your psyche and uncover the hidden parts of yourself that you may not even want to admit exist.

### House Cusps and Their Meaning

The eighth house's cusp points are the midheaven and the ascendant. The midheaven, also referred to as Medium Coeli, is associated with our public lives and our aspirations. It speaks to what we hope to achieve in life but also carries the potential for transformation and growth. The ascendant, or Imum Coeli, is related to your personal lives and how you interact with the world around you. It reflects your personality, how you present yourself to the world, and how you take in information from your environment.

### Main Keywords

The eighth house in astrology is associated with life's more complex and challenging traits. Transformation, growth, regeneration, and renewal are all keywords that reflect the constant cycle of change - but this house also covers taboos like mortality, death, and sex. Far from being an area to be overlooked, these themes provide a unique opportunity for a greater understanding of your life and how you interact with yourself and others. This can be a stimulating journey of mastery as you peel back the mysteries of the eighth house!

### Description of the House's Theme

The eighth house in astrology is a powerful and mysterious force. This house is all about transformation, challenging your beliefs, and exploring the depths of your psyche. It covers difficult topics such as mortality, death, and sex in a way that allows you to confront these areas of your life with understanding and acceptance. Despite the difficult nature of these topics, embracing the eighth house can be incredibly rewarding as it provides you with a greater understanding of yourself and your place in the world.

### Planet/Sign Analysis

The eighth house is ruled by Scorpio, which carries with it a sense of transformation and change. Although it may seem daunting, embracing the energy of Scorpio can allow you to explore your innermost desires and find a path to personal growth. The sign's strong connection with sex provides you with an opportunity to understand your sexuality better and what it means for you as an individual.

The ruling planet, Pluto, is all about power and control. It can be difficult to confront areas of your life that you may fear, but Pluto's energy gives you the strength to move forward. It also speaks to your ability to regenerate and find new life in the wake of death. By embracing Pluto's energy, you can find the strength and courage to confront and overcome your fears.

Ultimately, understanding the eighth house provides you with a greater insight into yourself and your journey in life. It allows you to confront difficult topics such as death and sexuality while at the same time providing you with growth opportunities. With its mysterious and powerful energy, the eighth house can be an incredibly rewarding area of astrology to explore.

## The Ninth House: Travel

The ninth astrological house is associated with knowledge, expanding mental horizons, and pursuing spiritual truth. It also focuses on the development of a better understanding of yourself and how you interact with the world around you. So, if you feel the urge to set off on an adventure and explore new places, physically or emotionally, perhaps it's the ninth astrological house whispering through your head! And why not? Experiencing different cultures has a way of broadening your perspectives, helping you learn more about yourself and others all at once.

The ninth astrological house is an area of focus that can bring great depth and meaning to our lives. It speaks to your sense of wonder and adventure and offers space for reflection and understanding. Travel teaches you about different cultures, exposes you to different perspectives, and enhances your ability to communicate with those you encounter.

Whether you are a globetrotter or a day tripper, this house brings forth opportunities for new experiences that you can take with you forever.

### Ruling Zodiac Sign and Planet

The ninth house is ruled by Sagittarius and its ruling planet, Jupiter. Jupiter symbolizes luck, expansion, and opportunity, all qualities essential for successful exploration. With Jupiter's influence, you are more likely to find luck and abundance on your travels, allowing you to be more open to new experiences and possibilities.

Sagittarius is the sign of exploration and knowledge. This sign encourages you to go beyond your comfort zone and seek out information that is different from yours. By embracing the energy of Sagittarius, you can become more open to learning and exploring, allowing you to return from your travels with a broader understanding of the world.

### House Cusps and Their Meaning

The ninth house cusp (Medium Coeli) is associated with the moon's south node and symbolizes your past. This point speaks to the experiences you have had in the past that shape your present and future. The Imum Coeli (the lowest point of the chart) marks the north node of the moon and speaks to your future. This point symbolizes potential and opportunity, showing you where you can go in life if you seize the chance. It encourages you to take risks, explore new possibilities, and make the most of your experiences.

### Main Keywords

The ninth astrological house is often said to be associated with luck, journeys, discovery, and the search for knowledge. Whether that means looking inward for spiritual truths or venturing out onto foreign lands and cultures, this house has something in store for everyone. You may never know the fullness of life, but with ongoing self-discovery and a curiosity for what lies beyond you, you can be sure that every moment is captivating. Exploring this incredible space can help reinvigorate your thoughts, broaden your perspectives, and open you up to new possibilities that you may have never anticipated.

### Description of the House's Theme

The ninth astrological house is a space for exploration and discovery. It encourages you to go beyond your comfort zones and seek out knowledge in all its forms. It speaks to your sense of wonder, curiosity, and ability to learn from the experiences you have had in life. With the ninth house, you can open yourself up to new perspectives, broaden your understanding and uncover the mysteries of life. The ninth house also speaks to your ability to make the most out of opportunities and take advantage of luck when it comes your way. Whether you find yourself on a new journey or simply exploring the depths of your mind, this house has something to offer you.

**Planet/Sign Analysis**

Jupiter in the ninth house offers us luck and abundance, encouraging us to go out and discover new things. When Jupiter is strong in your chart, you are more likely to experience success and opportunity on your travels. In the ninth house, Sagittarius encourages you to be open-minded and seek knowledge. This sign encourages you to question the status quo and learn from the experiences of others. When you embrace the energy of Sagittarius, you are more likely to open yourself up to new perspectives and expand your understanding of the world.

By exploring the ninth house, you can discover more about yourself and the world around you. You can open your mind to new possibilities and experience life in a way that you never thought possible. By diving into this space, you can find abundance and opportunity, allowing you to continue your journey of discovery for a lifetime.

The seventh, eighth, and ninth astrological houses offer us a tremendous chance to look further into our inner and outer worlds. These are the houses of relationships, growth, and travel, where you start to get in touch with yourself and how you connect with other people. From what it says about your deepest desires, revealing the way you grieve, or giving insight into your quest for success, understanding these three houses can give you a better understanding of yourself, your motivation, and how you navigate life. Even if you're unfamiliar with astrology, exploring these houses is an invaluable opportunity that can awaken amazing new things in you.

Each house is filled with its meaning, symbolism, and lessons, giving you a chance to uncover something new about yourself and your place in this world. By tapping into the energy of these three houses, you can open yourself up to a new realm of possibility and start to make sense of your life. With an open mind, a brave heart, and a willingness to explore, diving into the seven, eighth and ninth houses can be one of the most transformative experiences you can have in life.

# Chapter 9: The Houses IV. Career, Friendship, and Spirituality

Astrological houses are an exciting way to learn about yourself and your journey through life. These areas of a natal chart teach you about your character, how you relate to others, and what the future has in store. They can provide powerful insight into the paths you may take, allowing you to gain clarity regarding your decisions and potential outcomes. Exploring these astrological houses can be an interesting experience that gives you a better understanding of who you are and why certain situations manifest in your life.

This chapter will explore the tenth, eleventh, and twelfth houses of a natal chart. It will dive into each house to look at the ruling zodiac sign and planet, house cusps and their meanings, main keywords that describe it, and a description of the house's theme that goes in-depth on what it signifies. It will also look at the effects and lessons of each planet and the zodiac sign in the house. If you're looking to deepen your understanding of career, friendship, and spirituality in your chart, this chapter is for you.

## The Tenth House: Career

When it comes to making choices about your career, look no further than the tenth astrological house. This influential house gives us insight into our professional paths and provides hints as to which direction we should go. It's all about mapping out what you want to achieve while on this earth, no matter how big or small. The tenth house is filled with potential opportunities that could push you further than you ever thought possible. Take a few moments to read up on the tenth house and see what messages it has for you. Knowing yourself is key to finding success and happiness, so be sure to understand the knowledge it can bring before deciding which path you should take when investing in your career.

### Ruling Zodiac Sign and Planet

The tenth astrological house is ruled by both Capricorn and Saturn. These two powerful forces give you the necessary perseverance and determination to reach your goals. They also teach you important lessons about self-discipline, structure, and focus. Capricorn is the zodiac sign of career, and Saturn brings in a sense of authority and responsibility. Together, they provide you with the tools to make wise decisions regarding your career choices. The combination of these two energies brings stability, ambition, and wisdom.

The properties of the tenth house govern work-related matters like career decisions or public reputation. An individual's goals for success are given an extra boost when Jupiter travels through this house, as chances for personal advancement often arise during those times. With some discipline and hard work, this house provides a great opportunity to fulfill one's ambitions using the larger global framework available to us during these periods. The tenth house symbolizes a person's connection to the world around them and how they use it to create a legacy for themselves.

### House Cusps and Their Meaning

The tenth astrological house has two cusps, namely the Medium Coeli (MC) and the Imum Coeli (IC). The Medium Coeli (MC) is the point at which you reach your highest potential and signifies a person's career goals and aspirations. The Imum Coeli (IC) is the point at which you are most vulnerable and signifies the person's innermost fears and weaknesses. It is crucial to understand both cusps to gain a complete picture of the individual's career potential. The Medium Coeli encourages you to reach for the stars and strive for success, while the Imum Coeli reminds you of your limitations and helps you stay grounded in reality.

### Main Keywords

The main keywords that describe the tenth house are ambition, career progression, public reputation, and social status. This house is about taking risks and achieving success through hard work and dedication. It is also about understanding how to reach one's goals by taking into consideration the larger social frameworks available to them. The tenth house is where you go to find your purpose and make your mark on the world. It is also the place where you find out how to make a name for yourself and create a lasting legacy. The keywords related to the tenth house help you to focus your energy on reaching your goals and making a difference in the world.

### Description of the House's Theme

The tenth astrological house is a fascinating entity that symbolizes ambition and career progression in our lives. According to astrological beliefs, this house points to someone's social status and distinction in their chosen profession. It also reflects how individuals will find stability and satisfaction with their achievements, what goals they pursue, the focus they put into them, and the respect they receive from society. Such matters become increasingly important as someone strives to move up the ranks. You may not fully comprehend how someone's ambitions affect the cosmic plane, but the concept of the tenth house can certainly give you a better insight into the process.

### Planet/Sign Analysis

Capricorn brings with it an ambition that drives you to reach the top of your chosen profession. It also teaches you how to stay focused and disciplined with your goals, as this is a necessary part of reaching success. Saturn, on the other hand, gives you a sense of responsibility and structure. It encourages you to be accountable for your actions and to understand the consequences of your decisions. Together, these two planets provide you with a sense of focus and power that you can use to reach greater heights.

In conclusion, the tenth house is a powerful and influential one. It asks you to embrace your ambitions, determine your goals and strive for them with purpose and hard work. It also teaches you the importance of discipline, structure, and responsibility in your life. Understanding these concepts can help you to achieve greater heights in your career and ambitions. With the help of the tenth house, you can create a better future for yourself and achieve your dreams. In addition, the energies of the tenth house can help you understand your position in society and how you can use that to further your ambitions. It encourages you to take risks, use the global framework available to you and make your mark on the world. You can use this astrological house to reach new heights with hard work and dedication.

# The Eleventh House: Friendship

The eleventh astrological house is full of mystery, but one thing which is known about it is that it signifies friendship and social connections. This house serves as a reminder that having close friends and meaningful relationships encourages you to feel appreciated, creates enjoyable conversations, and promotes socialization. Furthermore, this astrological house emphasizes shared interests, support systems, and understanding in friendships. Whether you meet someone at college, during an outing, or even online, the eleventh house highlights the importance of building a strong connection with those around you so you can grow together in life experiences.

### Ruling Zodiac Sign and Planet

Both Aquarius and Uranus rule the eleventh house. Aquarius stands for progressiveness, innovation, independence, and friendship. It encourages you to be unique, creative, and non-conforming. Furthermore, Aquarius pushes you toward thinking outside of the box and embracing your individuality. Similarly, Uranus helps you make connections and explore your environment. It is associated with technology, science, and unconventional ideas that can help you to gain a better understanding of your surroundings.

### House Cusps and Their Meaning

The eleventh house cusps are between Aquarius and Pisces. The cusp of the eleventh house is associated with the theme of friendship and finding a sense of connection with those around you. As this house is associated with Aquarius, it can also be seen as the collective consciousness of the universe. It encourages you to think about your social and environmental environment and how you can work together to make a positive change in the world.

### Main Keywords

The eleventh astrological house is an exciting and expansive energy that is well worth exploring. It's a unique blend of friendship, collective consciousness, socialization, technology, science, progressiveness, innovation, and independence, all merging to form a distinct identity. Filled with curious potentials and possibilities that can often go untapped, the eleventh house encourages you to explore your creativity, seek out meaningful connections with others and stay open-minded toward the new dynamics unfolding in the world around you. With the right mindset and attitude, any individual working within this house has the opportunity to experience drastic personal growth and help shape a more progressive future for everyone.

### Description of the House's Theme

The eleventh astrological house is an interesting, creative, and expansive energy that symbolizes friendship and collective consciousness. This house encourages you to think outside of the box and explore your environment. You can use this house to connect with others, build meaningful relationships and open your mind to the new and innovative ideas which are constantly emerging in society. It is also a reminder that working together can make a positive change in the world and help shape a better future for all.

### Planet/Sign Analysis

Aquarius, the ruling zodiac sign of the eleventh house, stands for progressiveness, non-conformity, and innovation. Aquarius encourages you to think with an open mind and explore your environment more abstractly. It also helps you gain a deeper understanding of the world around you and embrace your individuality and unique perspective.

Uranus, the ruling planet of this house, symbolizes technology, science, and unconventional ideas. This planet helps you to make connections and understand your environment more creatively. It pushes you to think outside the box and come up with innovative solutions to your challenges. By exploring your creativity, you can make a positive change in the world and create a better, brighter future for everyone.

Going beyond your comfort zone can be daunting, but the eleventh house helps you do just that. This is where you discover new ideas and build relationships with others. You can engage with people and concepts which may have been previously unknown to you and open your mind in exciting ways. It's not easy doing something different or going out of your way to befriend someone new, yet it can be incredibly rewarding in the end. Why not take a chance and see what this amazing house has to offer? You never know what you may find!

## The Twelfth House: Spirituality

The twelfth astrological house is an interesting concept that often resonates with individuals looking to increase their spiritual awareness. It can serve as a map, guiding you on your journey to a greater understanding of yourself, the universe, and the divine. This house has always been associated with spirituality and offers spiritual growth through the exploration of the subconscious mind. By discovering your true intentions and goals, you strengthen your connection with the divine and are better able to recognize your true purpose in life. Through careful self-reflection, astrology offers you a gateway into deepening your spiritual practice, looking within yourself to find peace, joy, enlightenment, and, ultimately, transformation.

### Ruling Zodiac Sign and Planet

The twelfth astrological house is ruled by Pisces together with its ruling planet Neptune. These two aspects are closely intertwined, as they both represent spiritual transformation, the power of dreams and creativity, and a deep connection with the divine. Pisces encourages you to look within and better understand your spiritual nature. Neptune, on the other hand, helps you find peace and fulfillment by exploring your subconscious and emotional depths.

### House Cusps and Their Meaning

The twelfth house cusps are the Medium Coeli (MC), which is located at the top of the chart, and the Imum Coeli (IC) at the bottom. The MC is associated with your future goals and ambitions, helping you discover what you truly want in life and what drives you to achieve your highest potential. It also encourages you to go beyond your comfort zone and explore the unknown, opening up a world of possibilities. The IC, on the other hand, symbolizes your foundation and personal values. It encourages you to look into your past experiences to gain insight and understanding into your current reality.

### Main Keywords

Everyone has fascinating dreams and thoughts that come to them from time to time. However, what is truly remarkable is the prophetic wisdom you can receive from your unconsciousness. The twelfth house of astrology teaches you how to explore your deepest subconscious levels, develop spiritual awareness, and use creativity to shape your path toward transformation. As you open up to the mystic power of this area of your life, you begin to appreciate the infinite potential of spirituality and divinity which resides within you. It's easier said than done, but there's no greater journey than taking this plunge into your inner depths and discovering a world of everlasting possibilities.

### Description of the House's Theme

The twelfth house of astrology is a magical place that holds many secrets and mysteries. It speaks to the power of imagination, spirituality, and transformation. This house is deeply connected with the subconscious and offers you guidance on how to tap into the creative depths of yourself. Through careful self-reflection, spiritual practice, and exploration of your subconscious mind, you can unlock a deeper understanding of yourself and discover the true meaning of your life's journey. Ultimately, you can use this knowledge to create positive change in your life and the world around you.

### Planet/Sign Analysis

The power of Pisces and Neptune in the twelfth house is profound, as they bring you to a place of deep inner understanding. Pisces reminds you to look within and take an introspective approach to gain a greater understanding of your spiritual nature. Neptune helps you to dive into your subconscious mind, accessing the powerful energy that lies within. Together, these two planets help you to unlock the deepest mysteries of your subconscious and explore realms of creativity and imagination that are often left untapped. By learning how to use the energy of Pisces and Neptune, you can open up a world of endless possibilities and find true enlightenment.

Ultimately, the twelfth house teaches you how to open up to your spiritual depths, unlock creativity and imagination, and embark on a journey of transformation and personal growth. By embracing the vast power that lies within us, we can use our insight to make positive changes in our lives and the world around us. The twelfth house is a gateway to profound spiritual wisdom and exploration, allowing you to unlock the mysteries of your subconscious and access the divine power within. You can find true enlightenment and inner peace with careful reflection and spiritual practice.

The tenth, eleventh, and twelfth houses of astrology are profoundly powerful, offering you guidance on how to access your creative potential and embark on a journey of spiritual growth. Through careful self-reflection, creative exploration, and unlocking the mysteries of your subconscious mind, you can gain a greater understanding of yourself and uncover a world of endless possibilities. With the knowledge from these houses, you can use your newfound insight to make positive changes in your life and the world around you. Uncover the power of spiritual wisdom and discover your true potential by exploring these three houses. By doing so, you can find peace, enlightenment, and a greater understanding of yourself.

# Chapter 10: Putting It All Together: Your Birth Chart

Birth charts are an incredible tool to help you to better understand a person's character and life. By looking at the position of planets, luminaries, and other astrological points at the time of birth, you can get an overall sense of a person's essential nature as well as their more obvious traits and abilities. It doesn't stop there. Birth charts can be used to accurately predict events that might manifest in one's life, highlight any potential pitfalls, and suggest actions that could aid in the fulfillment of one's greatest potential. It can provide powerful advice, guidance, and words of caution for anyone who takes the time to immerse themselves in this fascinating science.

This chapter will provide a brief overview of interpreting and understanding birth charts. It will begin by defining what a birth chart is and its purpose. It will then take an example of a natal chart and discuss how to read, interpret, and draw potential conclusions from it. With the help of clear step-by-step instructions (including examples), you will better understand how to interpret the chart. The positions of planets, luminaries, and other astrological points within the chart matter greatly when interpreting birth charts. Signs, degrees, and intercepted signs on the chart can provide insight into relationships, work ethics, interests, and flaws.

# What Is a Birth Chart?

A birth chart is a symbolic representation of the sky as viewed from Earth at the time of someone's birth. It is a map of the sky at the specific moment and place of your birth, offering insight into the subconscious and spiritual qualities such as personality traits, emotions, and physical looks. In addition to psychological characteristics, it can be used to better understand career paths to pursue meaningful careers which are tailored to your unique profile. Taking an in-depth look at a birth chart can be incredibly revealing simply because they provide a focal point for understanding your life, including the past, present, and future.

# How to Interpret a Natal Chart

Interpreting a natal chart is a fascinating and rewarding experience since it can provide unique insights into an individual's personality. At its simplest level, a natal chart consists of various planets and points that are placed in a symbolic 360-degree wheel around the Earth. Using astrological principles, these positions can be read to reveal the potential and objectives of the individual.

First, you should look for major planetary patterns (such as trines or squares) to determine the energies which are conducive to how you interact with the world. Second, specific planet degrees will indicate particular qualities of life experience. Finally, pay attention to how the planets interact with each other - this can offer deep insight into yourself and your relationships. With practice, looking at your natal chart can unlock new layers of understanding!

### A. Degrees and Intercepted Signs

A natal chart is comprised of two core components, namely degrees and intercepted signs. Degrees are measured from 0°-360° and represent the position of each planet in the sky upon your birth. Meanwhile, intercepted signs are 12-fold divisions of a sign that only appear when certain planets occupy special features or when they occupy confined constellations. However, these trapped signs don't have any essential value unless planets are present to activate them, meaning you should never rely on intercepted signs alone. With these fundamentals in mind, you can start building your very own natal chart and deciphering the pieces that make up your personality.

### B. Relationship, Work Ethics, and Interests

Interpreting a natal chart can be a great way to learn more about yourself and what makes you tick. It can provide insights into your relationships with others, how you approach work, the lifestyle that suits you best, and even what interests you the most. There's no "right" or "wrong" way to interpret a natal chart. It's entirely based on subjective observations and intuitions. However, by using reliable information from an astrologer and carefully exploring all of the various aspects of your chart, such as planets and zodiac signs, an individual can begin to uncover valuable pieces of information about themselves. Whether you're just curious or in search of some serious self-reflection, learning how to interpret a natal chart is sure to bring major benefits.

### C. Flaws and Qualities

Interpreting a natal chart can be intimidating because of the amount of information available and the overwhelming range of flaws and qualities to analyze. However, with a few simple guidelines, you can approach it with confidence. Start by thinking broadly. A natal chart gives you an overview of personality traits and indicators, which may lead to understanding how planetary influences affect your life. A convenient way to make sense of this is to break down a chart into pieces and gauge the effects each snapshot has on your life.

Afterward, assess which qualities are either accelerating growth and development or causing challenges and challenges that need addressing. Finally, cultivate resilience when it comes to accepting any unfavorable outcomes from a natal chart. Keep in mind that all interpretations are subjective. Qualities, regardless of how unfavorable, can provide insight into how best to use strengths by focusing on gradually building weaknesses over time.

### D. Aspects and Transits

The natal chart is an essential tool used for astrological interpretation, commonly used for understanding one's personality and preferences. It utilizes the aspects and transits to tell a story about your place in the Universe. Aspects measure the angles between planets in the sky, while transits are what happens to them over time as they move through the sky from month to month and year to year. Understanding how to interpret a natal chart is the basis for gaining insight into the complex motion of planets.

Depending on which system you utilize, interpreting natal charts can encompass psychological analysis, zodiacal wisdom, or practical advice. Whatever your practice may be, studying a natal chart requires patience and dedication, as each individual's planetary movements are unique. With advanced knowledge of reading and using these tools, you can gain a holistic view of your life when you interpret your chart.

### E. The Rising Sign and Its Meaning

Interpreting a natal chart can be daunting, but understanding the basics of the rising sign can make it less intimidating. A person's rising sign is calculated based on the position of the sun and other celestial bodies according to their exact birth time and place. It's important to look at all of the components together to form an interpretation. While different signs have different energies, what matters more is how they interact with each other. The rising sign helps start this process by providing insight into someone's basic personality and characteristics in addition to other deeper layers of personality. Even though it is a complex topic, learning how to interpret a natal chart doesn't need to feel overwhelming if you break it down into digestible pieces and take your time.

## Tips and Tricks for Interpreting a Birth Chart

Now that you have a better understanding of how to read and interpret a natal chart, here are some tips to make the process easier.

### A. Look for Patterns

Looking at your birth chart is like putting on a detective's hat. By examining all of its components, you can start to build an understanding of the energies that inform a person's life. With practice, people can develop methods for analyzing and interpreting birth charts to get information about various aspects of one's life. The more time and effort invested in this study, the deeper your appreciation and understanding of it will become. Unexpected patterns sometimes appear among these symbols, helping to provide clarity on what is going on at any given moment in a person's life. Learning to read and interpret these patterns can be incredibly rewarding.

### B. Consider Sign Rulerships

Interpreting a birth chart can be a powerful practice for self-discovery. One of the most important components in birth chart interpretation is understanding sign rulerships. This means looking at which zodiac signs each planet rules and their corresponding astrological houses. For example, Mercury rules Virgo and Gemini, while Saturn rules Capricorn and Aquarius. When evaluating a birth chart, you can see how those planets impact different parts of the person's life based on the corresponding zodiac signs and houses. It's exciting to discover how the planets have influenced someone's life journey.

### C. Pay Attention to Any Fixed Stars on the Chart

When interpreting a birth chart, pay special attention to any fixed stars that appear on the chart. Fixed stars are points in the night sky that exhibit an influence over world events and individual lives. Among other things, a person's birth chart is determined by the positioning of these fixed stars at the time of their birth. Knowing where a particular star resides in a person's birth chart can enrich our understanding of their life path and karma, allowing us to draw more empowering insights from the same chart.

### D. Make Connections between Planets and Houses

Interpreting a birth chart can be a fun and insightful process. To start, you will need to get an overview of the key elements of a birth chart, including the planets and houses. The planets represent different energies and living areas that are believed to impact your life. These include inner planets such as the Sun, Moon, Mercury, and Venus, which symbolize our inner qualities and outward expressions, outer planets such as Jupiter, Saturn, Neptune, and Uranus, which are associated with larger patterns in your life, as well as Pluto and Chiron.

The houses represent parts of our life that are affected by these adventures. Each house has a particular focus, from relationships in the 7th house to career choices in the 10th house. Connecting these two ingredients will help you to gain insight into how planetary energies affect different aspects of life according to your birth chart.

### E. Keep an Open Mind and Notice the Details

Interpreting a birth chart can be an eye-opening journey for those eager to learn more about themselves. By delving deep into the details of their astrological chart, readers can gain powerful insights into their unique lives and personalities. While it is natural to feel cautiously hesitant, keep an open mind and be willing to accept whatever discoveries come your way. With each birth chart interpreted, you can come away with precious knowledge that can help you further understand and explore different facets of their psyche. Don't be afraid to let yourself dive deep, forget preconceived notions, and find out what truly resonates with you.

## F. Use Your Intuition to Develop a Symbolic Reading of the Chart

Interpreting a birth chart can provide you with deep insight into yourself and your relationships with other people. Drawing on symbols in your surrounding environment to create a meaningful interpretation of a birth chart is an incredibly valuable tool for personal growth and development. In most cases, the symbols used should have some connection with the person. That will add an extra layer of personal relevance to the task.

Harnessing the power of intuition and taking time to meditate upon the symbols chosen can be incredibly useful when interpreting a hybrid chart, allowing you to truly delve into each area of significance. Utilizing your natural senses and sensibilities will give you a renewed understanding of yourself, unlocking new realizations that could set you on an exciting path toward self-discovery.

## G. Consider Aspects and Their Meaning

Instead of viewing a birth chart as a fixed and predetermined meaning, it should be seen as an opportunity to consider multiple aspects of yourself and to discover creative possibilities. When you interpret your birth chart, use the information you glean as inspiration, identify the gifts and talents which show up, learn how the stars and planets influenced them, and how your chart can guide you in living your best life. With each part of the chart having its meaning, from the planets, signs, houses, and elements, take time to research and explore what each one brings to your individual story. You can use that knowledge to understand yourself better, change patterns of behavior that no longer serve you, and discover new pathways for growth opportunities, all with a greater sense of purpose.

Reading and interpreting a birth chart is one of the oldest forms of astrological study. By delving into its symbolic meaning, you can gain a greater understanding of yourself and your unique perspective on the world. While it can be an incredibly eye-opening experience, it is essential to remain open-minded and use your intuition to develop a meaningful interpretation. By taking time to consider aspects such as planets, signs, houses, elements, and their respective meanings, you can gain a unique insight into your own life and how the stars have shaped it.

# Extra: Astrological Symbols and Glyphs

A natal chart is a unique map of the sky at the exact moment you were born. It can tell you many things about yourself, and more often than not, a natal chart generated online will come with glyphs and symbols. While these images may seem daunting at first glance, have no fear. This final chapter will explain them in detail so that you can understand just what your natal chart means.

## Planet Glyphs and Symbols

Have you heard of planet glyphs and symbols? These symbols are believed to be used by civilizations outside of our own, including civilizations from other galaxies. Many scientists agree that these glyphs could tell a story about the lives of forgotten people who once inhabited certain planets scattered across the cosmos. They may even provide glimpses into what the future may hold for you. Understanding planet glyphs and symbols can be difficult, but gaining insight into them can be incredibly rewarding!

Here are the most commonly used glyphs and symbols for each planet:

- Sun: A circle with a dot in the center
- Moon: A crescent moon
- Mercury: A curve above a circle with a cross at the bottom
- Venus: A circle with a cross at the bottom

- Mars: A circle with an arrow pointing up
- Jupiter: A combination of two symbols, the crescent moon and the cross
- Saturn: A cross with a curl at the bottom
- Uranus: Two half circles with a cross in the middle
- Neptune: A trident
- Pluto: A small circle with a cross underneath

## Sign Glyphs and Symbols

Each sign of the zodiac has its unique glyph and symbol that can be used to represent it. These symbols have been used for thousands of years and can provide insight into a person's character, strengths, and weaknesses. From Egyptian hieroglyphs to Chinese pictograms and even modern-day road signs, these symbols have found their way into your everyday world and day-to-day life. They help you to navigate new places, and create an unambiguous understanding when using a language that isn't shared. Here are the glyphs and symbols for each sign of the zodiac:

- Aries: A ram's head
- Taurus: A bull's head
- Gemini: Two pillars
- Cancer: A crab
- Leo: A lion's head
- Virgo: A maiden
- Libra: Scales
- Scorpio: A scorpion
- Sagittarius: An archer
- Capricorn: A mountain goat
- Aquarius: Water bearer
- Pisces: Two fish

# Abbreviations

When reading a natal chart, you may see some abbreviations for certain important aspects of the chart. Here is a list of some of the most common abbreviations you may come across:

- MC: Midheaven or Medium Coeli
- IC: Imum Coeli or Nadir of the chart
- ASC: Ascendant
- DSC: Descendant
- Deg: Degree
- Hs: House
- PL: Planetary Ruler
- N. Node: North Node
- S. Node: South Node
- Chiron: The Wounded Healer

Now that you understand the glyphs and symbols used in natal charts, you have all the tools to interpret your chart. With this knowledge, you will have a much better understanding of the unique story in your very own natal chart.

# Conclusion

Astrology is an ancient practice that has had a resurgence of popularity in recent years! Each zodiac sign brings unique traits. The twelve signs represent the passage of the seasons and the position of planets at the time of birth. They can explain why you interact with others or yourself in certain ways. Tapping into essential energies related to each zodiac sign helps you find balance and better understand your cycles. All these aspects combine to form a detailed picture of your character.

Learning more about yourself through your zodiac sign, discovering you have a great affinity for certain traits, or uncovering a few habits that habitually cause issues in life can be a strangely gratifying experience. Everyone enjoys finding out more about themselves, and in the case of astrological signs, it can reveal dimensions to your personality that you never knew existed. With star signs divided into twelve categories based on the position of stars and planets at the time of birth, it becomes easier to understand why some things come naturally to you while others do not.

Astrology has been a part of countless cultures for centuries and remains one of the most intriguing aspects of human history. From Chinese astrology to Western zodiac signs, people have used this ancient system as a way to make important decisions and plan for the future. Technology has allowed people to access this knowledge in a matter of seconds instead of having to search through volumes of old texts or seek out an experienced astrologer.

With mobile apps and digital platforms, today's generation is privileged to have such an abundance of information at their fingertips. It's no wonder that astrology remains one of the most popular spiritual schools there. Take this informative guide, for example. It covered all the basics, including information on the planets, zodiac signs, houses, and asteroids. From the ego to home, career, and travel, every area of life is touched upon. It also provided an understanding of the symbols and glyphs used in astrology.

This book gives you a comprehensive view of the cosmic realm to help you make sense of this ancient practice and give you a chance to explore your birth chart. With the knowledge gained from this book, you can use astrology as a tool for self-growth and exploration. In doing so, you may find yourself better equipped to make important life decisions and form meaningful relationships. All in all, astrology can be a powerful guiding force in your journey toward self-discovery.

So, what are you waiting for? Start exploring your chart today and unlock the secrets to a more fulfilling life!

# Part 2: Birth Charts

*The Ultimate Guide to Natal Chart Interpretation, Astrology, and Zodiac Signs*

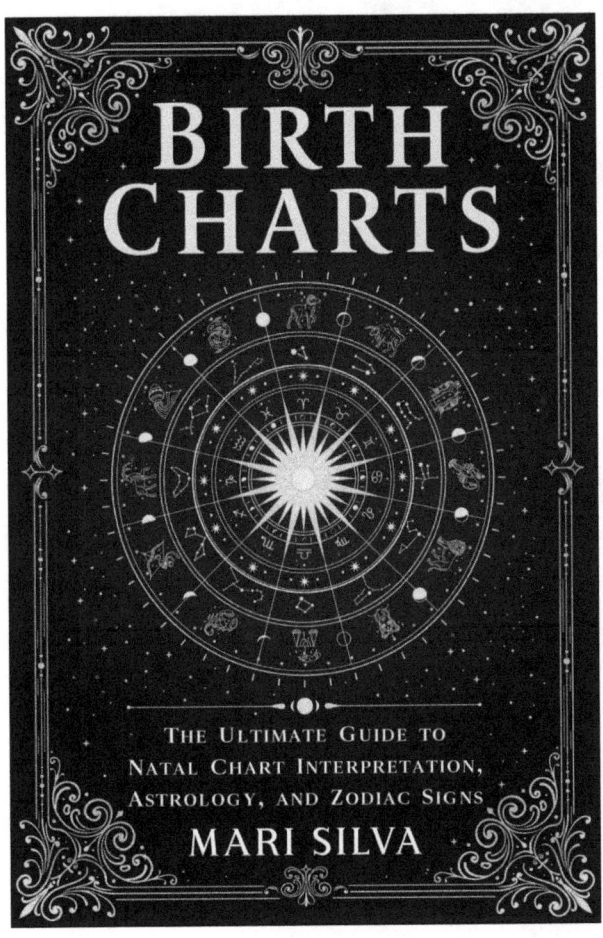

# Introduction

Have you ever felt as if you were living in the wrong time or wondered why you seem to clash with certain people while others just *get* you? Your birth chart might hold the answer. It is like a cosmic DNA test that reveals your unique qualities and quirks and helps you make sense of the world around you. Imagine having a roadmap to your innermost self, a blueprint of your strengths and weaknesses, your life purpose, and your growth potential. This is what a birth chart offers – a glimpse into the mysteries of the universe and your place in it.

Think of your birth chart as a personal guidebook to help you navigate life's twists and turns. It will not predict your future or make decisions for you, but it will give you a deeper understanding of yourself and where you fit in, in the world. With the help of this book, you will learn how to harness the power of astrology to live your best life and become the best version of yourself.

Astrology has been around for centuries, but it is only in recent years that it's gained mainstream popularity. Astrology has become ubiquitous in modern culture, from daily horoscopes to compatibility charts. But beyond the surface-level fun and games lies a deeper truth – the stars can reveal much about our lives and who we are. This book demystifies the complex world of birth charts and makes them accessible to everyone. Whether you're a skeptic or a believer, this book will take you on a journey of self-discovery and help you understand the singular cosmic imprint you had from birth.

What differentiates this book from other astrology books on the market is its focus on practical, hands-on methods. You won't find any dry explanations or complicated jargon here. Instead, each chapter includes clear language and step-by-step instructions to guide you through the process of creating and interpreting your own birth chart. With this book, you'll learn how to decipher the meaning of the planets, signs, and houses in your chart and how they interact with each other.

Whether you're a complete beginner or have some knowledge of astrology, this book will provide a thorough guide for anyone looking to explore the mysteries of the universe and gain a deeper understanding of themselves and others. So, get ready to embark on a journey of self-discovery and unlock the secrets of your birth chart.

# Chapter 1: What Are Birth Charts?

In this chapter, you'll learn everything you need to know before you embark on your birth chart reading journey. You'll understand what a birth or natal chart is, its significance, and its use. We explain why learning to read your birth chart can be empowering and how it can help you improve and transform your life. You'll also find out where the first version of the birth chart was found and its possible place of origin. Finally, you'll understand the key elements that make up a birth chart before you dive deeper into each of them in the following chapters.

## What Is a Birth Chart?

It's a snapshot or map of where the stars and planets were at the exact time and place you were born. If you look at a chart without knowing how to read it, all you'll see is shambles of symbols, lines, and characters. Birth charts have their own language, which takes a lot of time and effort to learn. However, learning to interpret yours, or anyone else's, is definitely worth the trouble!

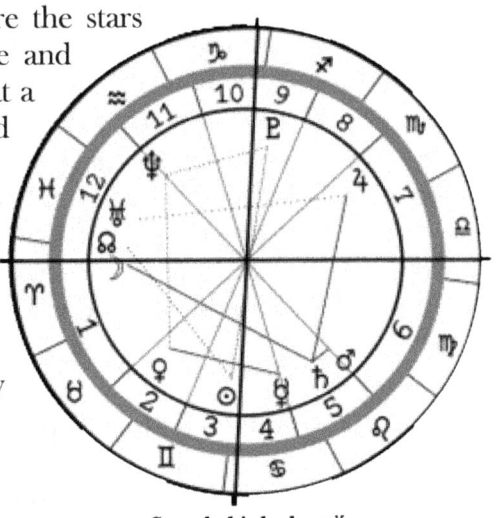

Sample birth chart.[14]

Just as a regular map gives you directions and scaled illustrations of the roads, bridges, rivers, fields, and mountains you'll encounter on your way there, your birth chart maps out your personality, key timings and events, and most importantly, your life's purpose. Knowing how to read it can give you insight into the paths you should take, when to act, and what you need to learn on your journey. Your birth chart lays out the endless possibilities and your interactions with the world as you embark on your life's mission.

The sky is always moving and changing- it never looks the same from one minute to the other. This is why the exact time of your birth is vital to a birth chart reading. If you haven't already, it's time to ask your parents or caregivers about your time of birth – or even request your long-form birth certificate from your birth hospital. You can still read your birth chart if you don't have the exact or even a rough idea about your time of birth. However, without this information, you won't know where the houses lie or your ascendant, which will be explored in the following chapter.

Your birthplace is also relevant to your birth chart because the sky looks different from different places. One person could be sunbathing while another stargazes on the other side of the world. Your birth chart is where you, space, sky, Earth, and time meet.

The most widespread depiction of the birth chart maps out the planets and the signs in the shape of a wheel. However, other traditions use shapes like squares to illustrate the birth chart. When reading a birth chart, you should pretend you're in its center. You need to step into the chart instead of reading it from above. This can be very confusing at first because once you're inside, the directions are flipped. The West is to the right, the East is to the left, and the North is South.

Each planet in space rules a different aspect of our lives and leaves a unique imprint on it. This means that all 12 signs influence certain areas of your personality and are relevant to certain parts of your life. Even if your star sign is Virgo, for instance, Scorpio would affect how you interact with your partners if Venus, the planet of love, is situated in that sign at the time of your birth. In that case, you'd be loyal and passionate toward your partner. You'd also bring sexual and intense energies to the relationship.

Your birth chart will look drastically different from someone who celebrates their birthday just a couple of days later. Even twins who were born minutes apart would have different birth charts. That said, some planets (Neptune and Uranus) and dwarf planets, like Pluto, change their location once every several years. They are, therefore, generational and can impact age groups as a whole. It's widely believed that 90s babies are more sexual than other generations because they were born when Pluto, the planet of sex, was in Scorpio.

Reading your birth chart can teach you valuable information about yourself. You'll understand why you behave and think in certain ways and have insight into the aspects of yourself that you need to work on. Your birth chart highlights all your positive traits, allowing you to capitalize on them. Each person sees the influence that astrology has over their fortunes in a different way. Many think astrology strips you of your sense of control because your path is already laid out. Another way of looking at astrology and how it impacts your life would be to think about it as a kind of warning or notice. For instance, the placements in your birth chart might suggest that you tend to become angry and have trouble building and maintaining healthy relationships. Instead of succumbing to your fate, you can change your life by actively managing your anger through mindfulness techniques or playing a sport. Knowing your problems brings awareness to them and what your triggers are, so you can take preventative action.

You'd also be surprised by the new revelations that come up when you re-interpret your birth chart. Once you get the hang of the craft, you'll need to return to it at different points in your life. Your birth chart always has more to offer – and you'll always find things you've missed previously, depending on what's currently happening in your life. It's also a refresher of things you overlooked and lost sight of over time. Some tendencies can become more pronounced during certain times of the year, and returning to your birth chart can remind you to reassume control.

The planets are always on the move. Your life will be affected in various ways as their placements change during the year. Unless you're up-to-date on these changes, you might be surprised that a significant transit or retrograde is influencing your feelings and behaviors.

One of the most popular examples of this phenomenon is the widely feared Mercury retrograde. Mercury is the planet of technology and communication and goes into retrograde three times a year. Suppose Mercury is situated in the house on your birth chart that affects your life at home. In that case, you might experience family problems or leaking roofs when it goes into retrograde.

# Where Did It Originate?

A research team discovered what is believed to be the oldest astrologer's board or preliminary version of the birth chart in a cave in Croatia right in front of the Adriatic Sea. This board is over 2000 years old and has engravings of zodiac signs, and is said to have been used to tell people's horoscopes.

The remaining part of the board has 30 pieces of ivory inscribed with zodiac signs in a Greco-Roman style. The researchers could recognize the symbols of Pisces, Cancer, and Gemini. The board was dug up near fragments of Hellenistic vessels and stalagmite fragments. Researchers explain that astrologers could've used the board to illustrate the sun, plants, and moon placements at the time of people's births. They also pinpointed the rising and setting points at the time of birth on the horizon. Not only is this discovery the oldest version of the birth chart, but it's also older than Greco-Roman written horoscopes.

There's still a lot of uncertainty regarding where the board was made and how it reached this cave. Babylonia was astrology's birthplace – around 2,400 years ago, people already had their own version of the horoscope. The science then traveled to the eastern Mediterranean, becoming very popular in Egypt. Since Egypt was ruled by a Greek dynasty at the time, the Greek style of astrology became the foundation of the practice.

On examination, archaeologists found that the ivory pieces used on the board are around 2,200 years old, which wasn't long before this style of astrology came into being. While they don't know for certain, researchers believe that Egypt could've been the birthplace of this board. The ivory came from a deceased or murdered elephant at the time. Being a very valuable material back then, the ivory could've been kept safe for decades – even centuries – before it was incorporated into the design of the astrologer's board. Some likely other symbols and elements were attached to the board that withered and disintegrated with time.

A trading ship might have taken the board and traversed the Adriatic Sea. Even though the Illyrians (the Croatian population at the time) weren't a subject of much interest to ancient writers, evidence suggests that they were involved in the Mediterranean world and engaged with the surrounding Greek colonies. With that in mind, an astrologer from a Greek colony would have traveled to Illyria to give readings and predictions. Even though giving a prediction in a cave under flickering lights would have been a transformative experience, it would also be impractical.

It's possible the Illyrians traded something in exchange for the board or stole it. The chances are that they didn't truly understand what it did but thought it looked valuable. The astrologer's board and the drinking vessels found at the site might have been placed as offerings to a deity – the cave could've also been a place of worship. The drinking vessels were very well-made and came from foreign lands. Archaeologists also found a few amphora vessels at the site. There's a possibility that worshippers brought wine and poured it into the newly acquired vessels, setting the amphora vessels aside because they weren't as good enough for the deity.

Even though the stalagmite probably formed naturally, it might have been the center of the offerings and rituals. It was phallic-shaped, and while researchers think that this detail could be of significance, many warn that all stalagmites look like that to a degree. Regardless of the meaning it symbolized to the worshippers, it almost certainly was a significant element in the cavern. Archaeologists suggest that anything the local community believed was valuable was taken to the cavern and offered to a transcendental force.

## The Key Elements in a Birth Chart

### Sun, Rising, and Moon Signs

Most people are familiar with their sun (star) signs, which is what they casually refer to or search for in their daily horoscope. The sun sign is representative of who you essentially are. The prominent constellation in the sky determines your rising sign at your time of birth. It reflects the traits you exhibit to the world and how others see you, especially when they're just getting to know you. Your moon sign is associated with your emotions. It relates to how you were nurtured in your childhood, your emotional needs, and what you need as an adult and in your relationships to thrive. Together, the sun, rising, and moon signs are commonly called "the big three."

### The Planets

For each planet, certain angles (ex: the rising sign is an angle) and luminaries (the Sun and Moon signs) represent various aspects of your life, personality, and outlook. Mercury, for instance, governs your thought patterns, listening abilities, and overall communication style. Venus is associated with how you express your affection, your innate sense of beauty, and how you relate to the world and others. Mars, the governor of sex, relates to your energy, sexuality, and proactivity.

While Jupiter is associated with your approach toward luck, good fortune, and abundance, Saturn determines how you deal with challenges, duties, restrictions, and important life lessons. Uranus is associated with your rebellious nature, Neptune rules your imaginative tendencies and dreams, and the dwarf planet Pluto rules transformative experiences and how you affirm your power.

Other key angles include the *Midheaven*, which is responsible for your destiny, fate, and professional image; the *Descendant*, which relates to your attitude toward partnerships; and the *Imum Coeli*, which is connected with your inner experiences.

### The 12 Zodiac Signs

All planets, key angles, and luminaries are situated in one of the 12 zodiac signs at the time of your birth. Their placement on your birth chart is associated with how the planet interacts with the sign and how this interaction influences your personality. For example, suppose Mars, the planet of proactivity, falls in Taurus, which is a steady Earth sign. In that case, you probably aren't impulsive and like to act at your own pace.

When you read your birth chart, you should also know that each sign is 30 degrees wide. Mars, for example, can fall at two degrees (or any other number of degrees), Taurus. You'll understand the significance of degrees when you learn about the aspects.

Even though any planet can fall into any sign, you should still consider the ruling planet of each sign while interpreting your chart. Learning that your Mars falls in Taurus gives you insight into how proactive you are, and understanding that Venus governs Taurus highlights your artistic side.

Aries, governed by Mars, is naturally playful, proactive, and competitive, and Taurus, which is ruled by Venus, thinks practically and pragmatically. Taurus is also sensual and likes all things luxurious. Gemini, which is administered by Mercury, is characterized by its quick-wittedness, curiosity, and good communication abilities. Cancer, ruled by the Moon, is unsurprisingly sentimental and nurturing, and it also actively seeks out a sense of security. The sun is the governor of Leo, making this sign optimistic, charismatic, motivated, and driven.

Governed by Mercury, Virgo is very sensitive and service-oriented. The sign is also known for its intellectual skills. Libra is ruled by Venus, is very sociable, enjoys partnerships, and is diplomatic. Scorpio is a unique sign-ruled by not one but two planets: Mars and Pluto. The sign is powerful, enjoys intimacy, and values its privacy.

Sagittarius is administered by Jupiter. It is an adventurous, free-spirited sign that speaks whatever comes to the heart and mind. Ruled by Saturn, Capricorn enjoys taking traditional paths. It is a hardworking sign that is driven by its ambition. Unlike Capricorn, Aquarius is very unconventional. Governed by Uranus, this sign is humanitarian and future-oriented. Neptune is the ruler of Pisces. Like its planet, the sign is highly imaginative and empathetic and partakes in spiritual endeavors.

**The Elements**

Each sign belongs to one of four elements: earth, fire, water, and air. Each element is associated with certain qualities and means of expression. For instance, fire signs are known for being proactive, while water signs lean into their emotions and intuitions. Air signs are sociable and intellectual; water earth signs are practical, organized, and natural-born planners.

The earth signs are Virgo, Taurus, and Capricorn, and the fire signs encompass Leo, Sagittarius, and Aries. The air element comprises Libra, Gemini, and Aquarius; the water signs are Pisces, Cancer, and Scorpio.

**The Houses**

The Houses are determined by the movement of the earth around its axis. This system is made up of 12 houses, each of which is connected to a certain theme or area of life. You can learn much about the events you experience and your direction by reading the house, planets, and signs they're situated in. Each house is ruled by one of the 12 signs.

These ruler signs differ from those that inhabit the houses on your birth chart. While the governor signs are the permanent inhabitants of each house, your personal house rulers are distinctive. The placement of your rising sign and the signs that follow is what determines how everything falls into place. Interestingly, those with an Aries rising sign will have sign-house placements that match up with the ruler of each house.

Aries rules the first house in the system and reflects your sense of self and ego. Taurus rules the second house, which is your income and possessions. The third house is ruled by Gemini and is associated with your communicative abilities and community. Cancer governs the fourth house and is concerned with your home and family life. Ruled by Leo, the fifth house is self-expression, creativity, and romance.

Virgo rules the sixth house and reflects your life's wellness, health, routine, and work areas. The seventh house is associated with your partnerships and is administered by Libra. The eighth house is the house of sex, emotional connections, death, and transformation and is ruled by Scorpio.

The ninth house is ruled by Sagittarius and is associated with philosophy, higher learning, travel, and adventure. Ruled by Capricorn, the 10th house has to do with your career and public image. The 11th house is technology, networking, friendships, long-term wishes, and humanity, and it is governed by Capricorn. The 12th and final house is ruled by Pisces and is associated with themes like psychic abilities, divination, spirituality, and the collective unconscious.

### The Modalities or Qualities

Each sign comes with its own quality or modality and can be fixed, cardinal, or mutable. Each modality carries four zodiac signs. The fixed signs, Taurus, Leo, Scorpio, and Aquarius, are usually stubborn and determined. The cardinal signs, Aries, Cancer, Libra, and Capricorn, are those that get a good headstart but find it hard to follow through with things. The mutable signs comprising Virgo, Gemini, and Sagittarius are highly adaptable.

### The Aspects

The five major astrological aspects are sextiles, squares, conjunctions, trines, and oppositions. They refer to the angles that the planets on your birth chart form and represent the relationships that every two planets have with each other.

If you have naturally compatible placements (such as fire and air) falling within three degrees away from each other, they're sextile. Unlike sextiles, squares are highly uncomfortable and challenging because they're formed when planets with incompatible energies are 90 degrees apart (such as water and air).

Two placements that fall in the same signs are considered conjunct and have a powerful influence on your personality. Trines are two placements with the same element, creating a sense of harmony. While oppositions are also challenging, they're less difficult to deal with than squares. They refer to planets that lie 180 degrees away from each other.

Now that you have read this chapter, you're ready to explore the upcoming chapters and explore these concepts in more depth. You should try learning all the glyphs by heart, as this will make reading any chart significantly easier.

# Chapter 2: The Astrological Houses I

When it comes to astrology, understanding birth charts and their interpretation can be overwhelming. However, one key element to focus on is the twelve houses in the chart. Each house represents a different aspect of life - from relationships to physical health, material wealth to spiritual beliefs. They each influence one another while being significant on their own level. While each house has its own function, they create an effective tool for prediction and analysis when blended together. The sun's ascending degree is also considered when deciphering how these houses should be interpreted in a birth chart. To further explain this concept, each house has a greater significance when paired with its accompanying sign of the zodiac yet remains vital individually. So, although confusion may arise when understanding astrological houses and their meanings in the context of a birth chart, with some knowledge, one can accurately interpret and understand these powerful aspects in guiding real-life situations.

## What Are Astrological Houses?

Astrological Houses are the 12 divisions of the sky in which a natal chart is divided. In astrology, they represent areas of life and the various stages of development that one must experience throughout their life. Each house is ruled by a planet, sign, and element, all of which influence how an individual experiences that house's topics.

The first house represents how an individual presents themselves to the world. It is associated with self-awareness, identity, physical appearance, and vitality. The second house looks at personal values, material success, and possessions. The third house focuses on communication, siblings, and neighborhood connections. The fourth house is concerned with home life, family dynamics, and emotional security needs. The fifth house addresses creative pursuits such as leisure time activities and romance. The sixth house looks at daily routines related to health, work schedule, and service to others.

The seventh house is linked with relationships, including marriage or business partnerships. It also examines how an individual interacts with others in terms of negotiation and compromise. The eighth house explores shared resources such as inheritance or investments along with death-related issues like legacies or grief counseling sessions. The ninth house covers higher education, long-distance travel, and spiritual exploration, while the tenth focuses on career goals and ambitions as well as public reputation matters.

The eleventh house centers around collective involvement within groups or organizations while exploring ways to manifest ideals into reality through collective action plans implemented by members within those groups. Finally, the twelfth house evokes introspection into dreams and subconscious influences while encouraging forgiveness of oneself or others who have inflicted pain in some way during one's journey through this world.

# Divisions of Astrological Houses

Zodiaque.

Zodiac houses wheel.[16]

## Quadrant 1- Personal Identity

### 1. First House

The first house in a natal chart is also known as the ascendant, and it represents the self – how someone presents themselves to the world and their physical characteristics. The ruling planet of the first house is traditionally considered to be Mars, with its corresponding zodiac sign being Aries. This indicates that traits associated with this house include instinctive action and assertiveness, impulsiveness, independence, courage, and strength. It also represents a person's sense of identity and purpose in life.

The keywords associated with the first house reflect its energetic nature and include creativity, initiative, leadership, competition, ambition, enthusiasm, risk-taking behavior, and confidence. These qualities are often seen in those with a well-aspected or dominant first house in their chart. Someone born with a strong presence of Mars in their chart will likely display more assertive characteristics than others who do not have an affinity with this planet. This may affect how they interact in terms of social boundaries and communication styles.

## 2. Second House

The second house in a natal chart is associated with material possessions, money, and the acquisition of wealth. It is represented by the sign of Taurus and is ruled by Venus, symbolizing desire and pleasure. This house also deals with your values, what you find pleasurable, your attitude toward possessions and money, as well as how you view material security. The main keywords associated with this house are abundance, resources, security, possessions, and values.

Understanding this particular house allows you to see how to relate your tangible assets and their impact on your life. Taurus represents being grounded and practical in terms of finances; it encourages us to maintain a steady flow of income while resisting impulsive spending habits. This can manifest itself through savvy investment decisions or the ability to save money without sacrificing the little pleasures in life. Furthermore, Venus' influence here speaks to the idea that having resources should not be seen merely as a means for survival but also enjoyed for pleasure's sake.

The second house is all about having a healthy relationship between you and your material possessions. It encourages you not to become overly reliant on material things, nor does it condone extravagance in exchange for security or comfort. Rather it suggests a balanced approach between thriftiness and enjoyment.

## 3. Third House

The third house in astrology is associated with communication, short-distance travel, siblings, and the surrounding environment. This includes your neighborhood and your relatives. Its ruling planet is Mercury, and its zodiac sign is Gemini. This implies that the energy of this house encourages inquisitive thinking, quick learning, small conversations, and gathering of news from close sources. It also encourages you to think outside the box, analyze details more closely, and make quick decisions when needed.

The keywords associated with the third house are communication, education, writing, reading, analyzing facts, decision-making skills, and adaptability. Being ruled by Mercury and Gemini gives us a natural ability to express ourselves through spoken or written words. You are easily aware of new information, which prompts you to think critically about your surroundings. Your communication style becomes more creative as you enjoy exploring different ways to express yourself through language or media platforms. You also begin to understand how important it is to speak clearly on matters, even difficult topics or sensitive subjects.

Overall, the third house represents how you can stay connected in our environment through education, facts, opinions, and adaptability to bring closer understanding between people - no matter their background.

# Quadrant 2 – Personal Expression

### 4. Fourth House

The fourth house of a natal chart is associated with the home, family, roots, and heritage. It rules over your innermost feelings, how you respond to your environment, and what kind of foundation your lives are built upon. Its ruling planet is the Moon, and its zodiac sign is Cancer. This implies that this house is deeply connected to one's emotions and intuition since Cancer is a sensitive water sign. The keywords for the fourth house include family, roots, childhood, security, safety, and nurturing energy.

When it comes to a deeper interpretation of the fourth house in astrology, it represents our psychological foundations - or how we were conditioned during childhood - as well as the environment in which we grew up. This can include physical home life, early family relationships, and those dynamics. It also speaks to the emotional security you feel in our everyday lives. Do you feel safe and secure? Are you able to express yourselves honestly? Do you have access to emotional support when needed? These questions can arise from looking at the fourth house of the natal chart.

The fourth house also speaks to matters related to inheritance - both materially (money or property) but also emotionally (how we process trauma) or spiritually (our relationship with that which is beyond us). All these elements make up an individual's unique sense of belonging, where they come from, and where they go. The fourth house helps provide insights into how one's past impacts their present situation and shapes their future trajectory.

## 5. Fifth House

The fifth house is associated with creativity, romance, and joy. It is symbolized by the Sun and is traditionally ruled by Leo, the sign of the lion. This house signifies entertainment, hobbies, children, and speculation. It also indicates risk-taking behavior and can be a source of inspiration for those looking to make changes in their lives.

When in a positive position on a birth chart, it brings optimism and enthusiasm for creative pursuits. It speaks of one's ability to take risks and express oneself artistically. One will have an open mind toward life experiences and seek new ways to express themselves through art or leisurely activities. This could be expressed through taking up painting classes or engaging in music lessons after work.

The keywords that describe the fifth house are enthusiasm, creativity, passion, freedom, risk-taking, playfulness, pleasure-seeking behavior, emotionality, and joyousness. It is the realm of love affairs and physical pleasures. As such, it speaks of our ability to attract others through love or even money through gambling or investments.

In terms of its associations with children, this house reveals how parents will nurture their offspring while instilling positive values simultaneously. Therefore it demonstrates how successful you will be in raising their children and creating meaningful relationships with them. This house also indicates how much joy you will experience from your children.

Overall, this house symbolizes everything that brings us pleasure. Whether through physical activity or creative activities such as playing an instrument or painting, this area represents what gives you happiness in life, so it should not be taken lightly when consulting one's natal chart!

## 6. Sixth House

The sixth house in astrology is associated with health, work and service, and personal development. It is ruled by the zodiac sign Virgo, which is an earth sign that values practicality and organization. This house also has a crucial role in the natal chart, representing our physical body and its condition.

The primary keywords for the sixth house are health, hygiene, diet, work ethic, discipline, responsibilities, routines, and self-care. These terms all relate to taking care of ourselves on a physical level. This can include maintaining good hygiene habits such as frequent handwashing and showering, eating healthy food, developing strong work ethics by showing up on time and being reliable, following disciplinary routines that help us to stay organized, and doing whatever it takes to take care of ourselves holistically. All of these aspects come together to form one's overall health picture.

When Virgo rules this house, it implies that you are detail-oriented and organized. It also means that you tend to be neat in your appearance and environment, which helps them achieve better physical health. Such people are often quite focused on getting things done right the first time around since they don't like to waste time or energy unnecessarily. Furthermore, those whose sixth house is ruled by Virgo will likely prioritize cleanliness in their daily and professional lives.

In addition to Virgo ruling this house, Mercury also influences this area of life significantly as it relates to communication skills and our ability to be resourceful with whatever we have at our disposal to solve problems efficiently. Those who possess strong Mercury energy will be able to think quickly on their feet in order to get things done quickly yet still effectively without becoming overwhelmed or overworked in the process.

Overall, the sixth house expresses our attitude towards ourselves by maintaining our physical well-being and caring for our professional commitments. It also reflects how you approach tasks that require mental discipline so that you can stay productive even when faced with challenging tasks or situations that require extra effort from us mentally or physically.

## Quadrant 3 – Relationships

### 7. Seventh House

The seventh house, ruled by Libra, is all about relationships and the give-and-take between two people. This house involves marriage, partnerships, contracts, legal matters, and business agreements. It's also called the House of Open Enemies because it deals with how you interact with your enemies. How you negotiate and compromise on issues are key points here. This house also reflects how well you handle confrontations with others and how good your public image is.

As for the ruling planet of this house, Venus is credited for its influence. Venus is known as a planet of love and beauty, and when it comes to the seventh house, it helps bring harmony to any given relationship or partnership. The sign associated with this house is Libra which represents balance and justice. Combined, these two influences help bring peace even if there are disagreements or opposing sides regarding a situation or issue.

The keywords that best describe the seventh house include relationships, partnership; marriage; beauty; harmony; balance; justice; negotiation; compromise; public image; confrontations, and agreements. These words illustrate how much importance this area holds in your lives and how it can be used to create successful relationships, both personal and professional. By understanding this house better, you learn valuable lessons that allow you to have more satisfying life experiences, particularly when dealing with others who may differ from us in opinions or beliefs.

## 8. Eighth House

The eighth house is a powerful and often misunderstood sector of a natal chart. It is ruled by the zodiac sign Scorpio and its ruling planet, Pluto. This house can be considered our "darker" side, as it deals with deeper psychological issues, such as death, inheritance, sex, and power dynamics between individuals.

The keywords associated with the eighth house are transformation, intense emotions and sexuality, rebirth and renewal, secrets and secrets-keeping, joint resources (such as finances or insurance policies), occult knowledge or practices, psychic powers, and intuition. These themes reflect the intensity of Scorpio. They are not necessarily negative in nature but represent forces requiring careful navigation.

This house reflects how you approach your deepest fears and desires. It speaks to our capacity for personal growth through transformative experiences. It symbolizes the challenges beyond your control that you face when dealing with difficult conditions in life. These challenges can lead to profound insights about yourself if you dare to confront them head-on. You may even find strength in them if you use them as learning opportunities for self-development.

The eighth house also reveals your ability to trust others with intimate secrets or valuable resources. This speaks to your ability to form meaningful bonds with people based on mutual understanding and respect. In partnerships of all kinds (romantic relationships included), this house holds great importance, as it reflects our willingness to share ourselves fully with someone else while maintaining healthy boundaries to protect each other's interests.

This house can often indicate blockages or unresolved issues from past lives, which can manifest themselves in physical or emotional ways throughout an individual's life. It is, therefore, necessary to pay attention to any patterns you observe before making decisions that could be potentially damaging! Finally, it is also worth noting that this house is closely linked with psychic ability and intuition; those who tend to be more psychically sensitive may find themselves looking towards the Eighth House when seeking guidance from their higher self or spiritual guides.

## Quadrant 4- The Social Expression Quadrant

### 9. Ninth House

The ninth house is associated with the sign of Sagittarius, and its ruling planet is Jupiter. This house suggests expansion, growth, exploration, journeys, and education. It encourages you to learn about different beliefs and cultures and to broaden your horizons. It also relates to laws and higher principles, both religious and secular. The main keywords that describe the ninth house include intuitiveness, morality, wisdom, philosophy, faith, higher education, and long-term goals.

Jupiter's influence in the ninth house means it helps you expand your understanding of ourselves and the world around us. You can gain life-altering insights through your travels or spiritual pursuits. Through learning new things, we can align our beliefs with our deepest values and discover how we fit into the grand scheme of things. The ninth house allows us to explore these concepts in a safe environment while granting us greater freedom in who we become as people.

On a deeper level, the ninth house reveals how you see reality and seek truth in life experiences. You receive guidance through introspection as well as seeking out teachers or teachings that resonate with you on a spiritual level. This house allows you access to inner knowledge, which brings forth greater clarity when it comes to difficult decisions or situations in life.

The energy of this house asks to embrace change with enthusiasm rather than fear because it's only through taking risks that true growth occurs. By pushing past your comfort zone, you can discover hidden depths within yourselves beyond what you have previously imagined was possible.

## 10 Tenth House

The tenth house of the natal chart governs your public persona, reputation, and career. It is associated with working hard to reach the top. Someone with a strong 10th house will be ambitious, industrious, and determined to leave their mark on the world. They will be highly organized and disciplined in their approach to life, setting goals and creating plans that they stick to in order to achieve success.

The keywords associated with this house are career, ambition, status, recognition, honors, and responsibility. People who have many planets in this house may take on a more authoritative role in their field or strive for recognition from others for their accomplishments. They may also have an urge to significantly impact the world or have a deep sense of duty toward achieving something meaningful.

The tenth house is known to bring workloads that require consistent effort over time; it is not uncommon for those with placements here to be burdened by too much responsibility at once due to their ambition. Someone with this configuration must remember that it's okay to take breaks to avoid burnout or neglecting other parts of life, such as relationships or hobbies, due to excessive focus on work-related matters. All in all, people with strong tenth house placements often find great rewards through hard work and dedication but must remember that there needs to be a balance between working hard and taking care of oneself at the same time.

## 11. Eleventh House

The eleventh house is crucial in your natal chart. It is ruled by the planet Aquarius and the zodiac sign of Aquarius. This means this house represents humanitarianism, friendship, hope, and wishes. The keywords associated are individual self-expression, higher mental levels, communication, truth, spiritual goals, and aspirations.

This house is about connecting to a larger purpose and helping others around you. The eleventh house encourages us to step out of our comfort zones as we connect with friends, causes, and clubs that help benefit society as well as yourselves. By connecting with others on a deeper level and exploring your spiritual side, you become more connected to your potential for growth and understanding.

When looking at the eleventh house in a natal chart, it can be helpful to think of it as a representation of the need for harmony between yourself and those around you. It's about understanding how your actions affect others and seeking ways to better keep things in balance within your relationships. This can often be done through communication or finding joy in activities that create unity among people, such as art, music, or meditation.

Your dreams can become a reality under the Aquarian influence because this house works to bring power into the Universal Mind through collective efforts toward spiritual pursuits. Working towards these goals will also give rise to new thought processes, allowing you to expand your mental horizons even further than before. Aquarius ruling this house encourages people to recognize the importance of truth when dealing with matters that could benefit all areas of life if utilized correctly.

### 12. Twelfth House

The twelfth house is the last and most mysterious house of the astrological natal chart. It rules over secrets, sorrows, and subconscious patterns. Pisces rule it, and its ruling planet is Neptune—the planet of dreaming, foggy boundaries, and illusions. This placement speaks to a person's hidden strengths and shadows. It is associated with the past, unconscious motivations, inner transformation, deep emotions, and seclusion. The keywords for this house are introspection, surrendering to the unknown, self-reflection, solitude, and unfulfilled desires.

This house helps you see beyond your rational mind and understand what lies underneath. It shows your deepest fears and hidden potential that may be difficult to access in everyday life. Its energies can also represent unresolved issues from childhood or other past experiences that continue to manifest in one's present reality. With this house comes a deep understanding that we all have something unique to offer, even if it's hard to accept at times.

Pisces energy brings forth unconditional love and compassion for yourselves as well as others around you, but it can also lead to escapism through addiction or avoidance behaviors if not used properly. The positive aspects of this placement are finding solace within oneself while connecting with your spiritual side—realizing there's beauty in mystery and pain. Being able to tap into creative ideas, learning how to forgive yourselves and others without judgment; coming up with solutions on both a conscious and subconscious level; taking a step back when need be; understanding that everyone has their own struggles, even if they don't express them outwardly.

# Chapter 3: The Astrological Houses II

Astrological houses are a significant component of a birth chart. They indicate our life's purpose, challenges, and potential growth opportunities. Astrological house systems are the way astrologers arrange the twelve houses of a horoscope, and each one looks at the same information from different angles.

The most commonly used astrological house system is Placidus, which astronomer Placidus de Titus developed in the 17th century. This system divides the zodiac into 12 equal 30-degree segments based on each individual's exact time of birth. It assigns each segment to one of the 12 zodiac signs and 12 houses, creating a circle of houses around the birth chart. Each house is linked to one of the planets, and its placement in the chart indicates which area of life will be most influenced by that planet.

The Equal House system is another popular astrological house system. This method divides the zodiac into 12 equal segments of 30 degrees each and assigns them to one of 12 astrological houses. The ascendant, or rising sign, marks the starting point for this system, so it's necessary to know your precise time of birth when using it. Unlike Placidus, no house is associated with any given sign; rather, every house has equal influence from all signs. This system is popular among astrologers for its simplicity, but many argue that it doesn't accurately portray the house placements in a chart.

The Porphyry System of astrological house division assigns different sizes to each house depending on the time of birth. This system divides the zodiac into 12 unequal segments based on how long it takes for each sign to pass through your ascendant point. The houses closest to the ascendant point are larger than those further away from it, and each house is associated with one specific zodiac sign. Some astrologers believe this method gives more accurate results because it accounts for the changing speed of signs at different times of the day.

Finally, there is the Koch System, which German astrologer Wilhelm Koch developed in the 20th century. This system divides the zodiac into 12 unequal segments of varying sizes, but the ascendant point still marks the start of each house. As with Porphyry, each house has an associated sign, and the houses closest to the ascendant are larger than those further away from it. The Koch System is believed to be more accurate than Placidus because it takes into account a wider range of factors related to time and space.

The various astrological house systems can help us better understand our birth chart and what lies ahead for us in life. By looking at our chart through different lenses, we get a deeper understanding of our personality, potential, and life's purpose that we may not have seen otherwise. Ultimately, it's up to the astrologer to decide which system works best for their interpretation style.

Regardless of which system you use, studying your astrological houses can help you get to know yourself better and what lies ahead. Have fun exploring!

## Ecliptical House System

The Ecliptical astrological house system is a method of dividing the sky into 12 portions or houses. It assigns each house to a zodiac sign, then divides it into 30° arcs. This system assigns astrological significances to each house, and the position of planets in these houses provides valuable insight into an individual's characteristics and life path.

The ecliptic is an imaginary circle in the sky that traces the annual orbit of the sun around Earth from our earthly perspective. As such, it has been used since ancient times as an important part of many cultures' astronomical and astrological practices. The zodiac signs are all positioned along this ecliptic path, which allows for further interpretation based on where planets fall relative to one another along its course.

When using an ecliptical astrological house system, certain points within this celestial arc are assigned significance depending on the interpretation one tries to make. Each house governs different areas such as home life, health, and finances; for instance, when interpreting a person's chart using this system, if there are planets in the fourth house, this could indicate family or domestic life issues. Depending on which side of the ecliptic they appear, positive or negative implications can be derived from their placement.

Furthermore, looking at how two planets relate to one another in a particular person's chart – known as aspects – can also provide more detailed information about how those two energies interact within their individual lives. An aspect is created when two planets fall within a certain number of degrees away from each other along the ecliptical path; for example, if two planets were placed 15° apart, they would create a trine aspect, which generally signifies ease and ease of harmony between those energies.

The ecliptical house system differs from both spatial and temporal house systems because it does not use actual physical locations to divide up the sky. Instead, it relies on the relative positions of stars and constellations within the sky itself at any given time. Furthermore, while both temporal and spatial systems require exact data points to make a precise reading, such as a specific location or date/time to accurately assess one's astrological position, the ecliptical system only requires a general idea of where stars/constellations are located relative to one another. This makes predicting one's life path or character traits easier than other methods.

Unlike temporal systems, which measure time-based changes within an individual's life path (such as age or each passing year), ecliptical systems measure long-term changes based on cosmic patterns that occur over larger timespans, such as decades or centuries. This process gives more insight into how cosmic forces affect long-term trends and patterns rather than short-term fluctuations that may be seen with temporal systems.

# Whole Sign House System

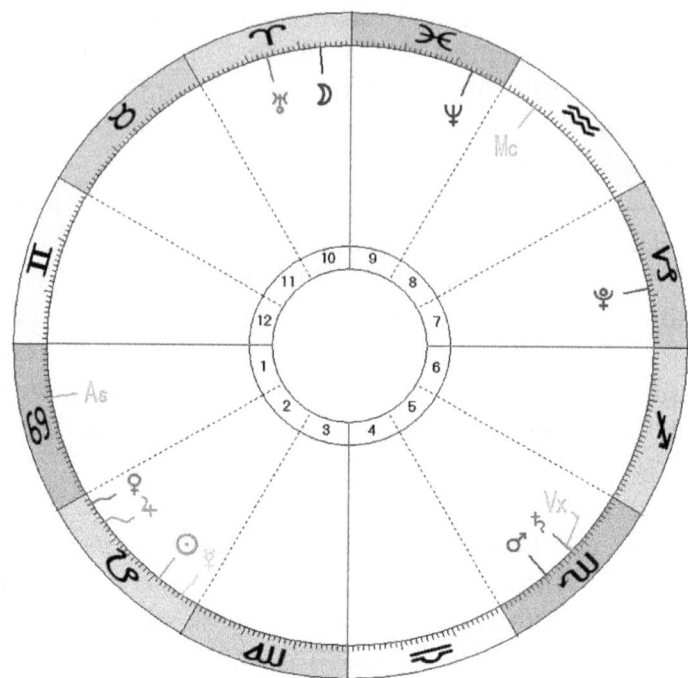

Whole Sign House divisions.[17]

The Whole Sign House system is an ancient and traditional method of calculating the 12 houses used in astrology. It divides the zodiac into 12 equal 30-degree segments, with each segment representing a different area of life and its associated themes. This method is based on whole signs, meaning it takes the sign that contains the ascendant (the point at which a person's chart begins) as the starting point of all houses. For example, suppose a person's ascendant falls within Aries. In that case, the first house will be located entirely within that same sign.

A birth chart using this plan would look like a wheel divided into 12 sections, with each section corresponding to one of the twelve astrological houses. The ascendant would be located in whatever sign corresponds to the first house, and all other planets throughout their respective zodiac signs would fill in each subsequent house. The main advantage of Whole Sign Houses is that it allows for a consistent measure across all charts regardless of where the ascendant falls – everyone will always have an entire house located within one sign.

The pros and cons of using this way when interpreting a birth chart depend largely on personal preference. On the one hand, Whole Sign

Houses are easy to understand and are consistent between readings even when comparing charts with different ascendants; however, they do not account for changes in declination or cuspal placements which offer additional insight into how certain areas of life might be expressed or experienced. Additionally, some astrologers find them too broad or generic when providing interpretations since they do not consider specific movements or placements within each sign. Ultimately it comes down to which method works best for you.

## Spatial System

Spatial astrological house systems are a way of interpreting the positions of the planets within our solar system and how they relate to events happening in our lives. This is done by dividing the sky into twelve equal "houses" or sectors, each associated with a particular area of life. The houses are numbered counter-clockwise from zero to 11, starting at either the ascendant (the point where the ecliptic and horizon intersect) or the midheaven (the point directly overhead). Each house then represents a specific aspect of life, such as health, career, family, finances, etc.

The position of each planet concerning these houses is then interpreted to see how that particular planet's energies will affect matters related to that house. For example, Venus's proximity to the seventh house may indicate increased relationships and social activities. Alternatively, if Saturn is near the fifth house, this could suggest difficulties with trying to pursue creative and leisurely activities.

Spatial astrological house systems differ from ecliptical and temporal house systems in several ways. In ecliptical house systems, the planets are placed into houses by measuring their position relative to the celestial equator, while temporal house systems measure their positions relative to the vernal equinox. However, spatial astrological house systems measure planets' position relative to local horizons and angles based on an observer's geographical coordinates. This allows for more precise placements of planets within different areas and also allows for a better understanding of how those placements affect one's natal chart interpretation as it relates to their specific location on Earth.

In addition, spatial astrological house systems may also account for variations in daylight savings time or changes in longitude or latitude due to travel or other changes in environment when calculating birth charts. This helps ensure that accuracy is maintained even if there have been changes since birth or relocation after birth. As such, this system offers far greater precision than either the ecliptical or temporal house system can provide, making it the ideal choice for people looking for personal exploration or spiritual development.

## Porphyry system

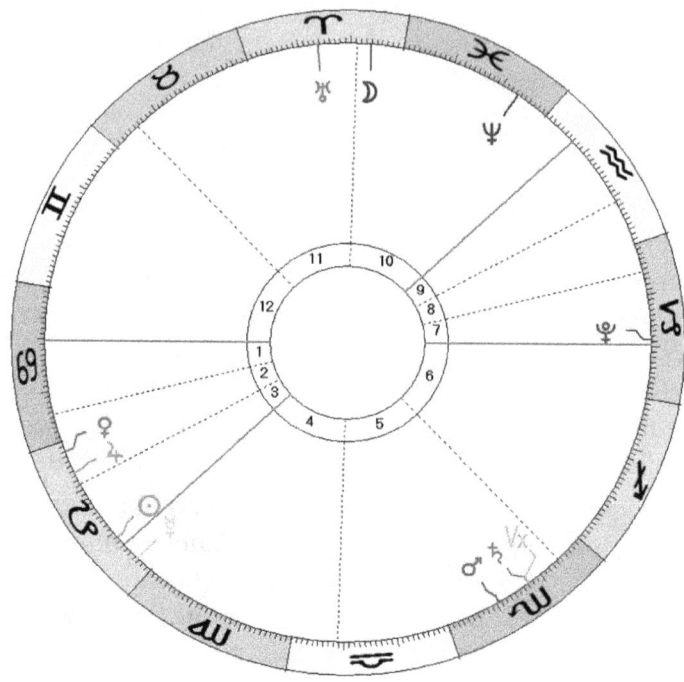

Porphyry house divisions.[18]

The porphyry system is a spatial house system that divides the celestial sphere into twelve equal divisions, each representing one of the twelve astrological houses. It was named after Porphyry, an Ancient Greek philosopher and astrologer who developed the system in the 3rd century AD.

At its core, the Porphyry system divides the celestial sphere into four quadrants, with each one measuring 30 degrees of longitude. The four points that mark these divisions are known as cardinal points, and they are fixed relative to Earth's position at any given time. The remaining eight house cusps can be calculated using trigonometry from these cardinal points. Each house is then divided into three subdivisions: decanates, which measure 10 degrees of longitude; terms or bounds, which measure two-and-a-half degrees of longitude; and faces, which measure five degrees of longitude. This gives a total of 36 sub-divisions for each house.

The birth chart created using the Porphyry system would be a circle divided into twelve sections, each representing one of the twelve astrological houses. There would be no unequal houses as in other systems like Placidus, nor will there be different placements for planets depending on their declinations from the ecliptic plane as in Equal House System or Koch System. The chart will have its Ascendant placed at zero degrees Aries and remain constant regardless of time and place, making it easier to interpret by delineating planets' positions in various houses, but it also has limitations as its interpretation does not take aspects between planets or their declinations into consideration while making predictions/interpretations.

**Pros:**
1. **Easy to Interpret** – Since the Porphyry system does not consider planetary declinations when creating a chart, it makes it easier to interpret the placement of planets in different houses without having to adjust for declination variations which can make charts difficult to read, especially for beginners.
2. **Constant Ascendant** – With the Porphyry system, the ascendant remains unchanged regardless of time and place, making it easier for astrologers to compare different charts with the same ascendant placement instead of having to adjust them before comparing.
3. **Simplicity** – Porphyry System is a fairly simple system compared to others, such as Equal House System or Koch System, where calculations become more complicated as they consider planetary declinations when calculating cuspal positions, thus making them difficult for beginners/ amateur astrologers unless they use software.

**Cons:**
1. **Limitations** – The Porphyry system ignores planetary declinations while calculating cuspal positions. This means that no aspect between planets or effects- due to their declination – can be considered while interpreting charts. This system thus limits the accuracy and precision of the readings.
2. **Time Difference** –Although the ascendant stays fixed, it does not adjust for the time difference between places, resulting in an incorrect determination of midheaven, especially if the interpretation is made by someone who is not in the same place *where the chart was created.*

Overall, the Porphyry system still offers many benefits, such as simplicity, easy readability, and constant ascendancy, making it a popular choice for beginners and amateur astrologers looking for simpler but accurate methods.

## Temporal House System

Temporal astrology is an ancient form of charting the movement of planets, stars, and other celestial objects through time. It uses a system of houses or zodiac signs to divide up the sky into 12 sections. Each house has a set of associated characteristics, which are then used to interpret the influences and events in a person's life at any given time. The most commonly used systems are Placidus and Campanus.

In astrological house systems, the exact placement of the planets concerning each other is crucial to accurately predicting events such as births and deaths, beginnings and endings, and successes and failures. This means that if a certain planet is found in a particular area of the sky, it may indicate something happening at that time or in the near future. For example, if Mars is situated in the fourth house at birth, this could indicate that there will be some kind of conflict or challenge when it comes to relationships with family members or close friends.

The strength and duration of the planetary patterns can also play an important role in temporal astrology interpretations. When two planets appear together for a period within one sign or house, it indicates a strong connection between those two aspects represented by those planets. These energies may bring about opportunities for growth or transformation depending on how they interact with each other. At times when multiple planets appear together in one area, this could also signal increased intensity as these planets all strive for dominance during their shared residence.

# Koch System

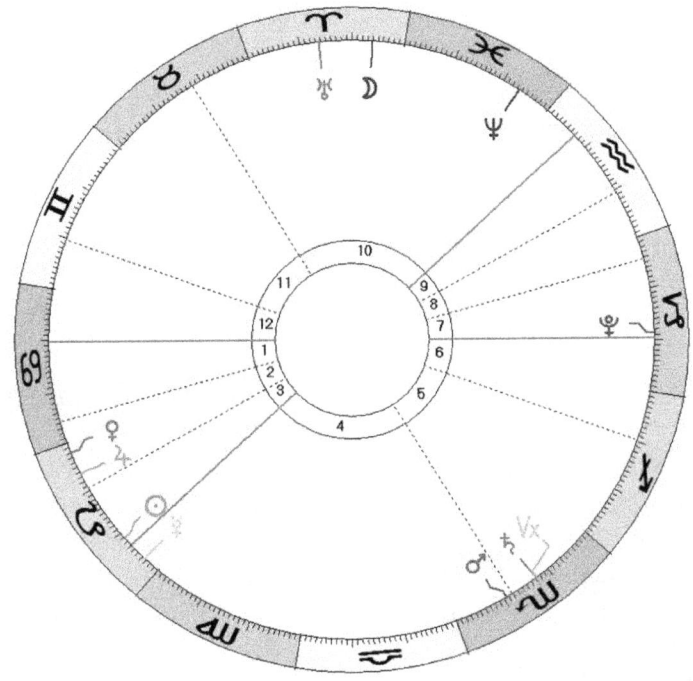

Koch house divisions.[19]

The Koch system is one of the most widely used in astrological interpretations. It is also known as the "temporal" house system because it takes into account the exact time of birth to determine a person's natal chart.

The Koch system differs from other house systems by using a mathematical formula based on a person's precise time of birth. This formula then determines where each planet falls within the 12 houses. Basically, the Koch system starts with an ascendant or rising sign placed at 0° Aries, considered the first house in any chart. Each consecutive house is then determined by calculating 30° from the previous one, with all angles being measured from the point of the ascendant. For example, if a person was born at 10 am on July 8th, then their rising sign would be placed at 0° Aries, and each subsequent house would be calculated from there; house two would begin at 30° Aries, House three at 60° Aries, and so on until all 12 Houses have been calculated.

A birth chart using this system would include all twelve houses beginning with 0° Aries representing the first house and ending with 29° Pisces representing the twelfth house. The planets would appear in order along these houses; however, they may vary depending on how close they are to each other or how close they are to a changing degree mark (such as 29°).

The primary benefit of using this method is that it considers how individual moments can differ slightly from one another when determining planetary placements and what those placements mean for that person's life. This allows for more accurate readings than other methods that don't factor in the small differences in positions. Additionally, because this method requires an exact time of birth, it gives more detailed information about specific timing-related aspects such as transits and progressions, as well as other intricacies in a person's chart.

On the downside, however, calculating planetary placement within each house can become quite complex under this method due to the varying degrees between planets or signs, so individuals who wish to use this method should have some basic knowledge about astrology before attempting any sort of interpretation. Additionally, many astrological software packages do not support this methodology, so individuals may have difficulty accessing certain features or data when working under this particular system.

**Placidus System**

The Placidus system is one of astrology's most commonly used temporal house systems. It was developed by the seventeenth-century French astrologer Placidus de Titus and was first published in 1683. This system uses a method called "whole sign houses" to divide the celestial sphere into twelve sections or "houses" based on the ascendant (the degree rising on the horizon at birth). The Placidus house system assigns each house an equal width, with no overlap between houses. This means that each house has a specific and independent meaning for interpretation purposes.

A birth chart using the Placidus system would typically look like a circle divided into 12 parts, each corresponding to a certain area of life, such as relationships or career. The ascendant (or rising sign) is usually positioned at the bottom of this chart and marks where the Sun was located at birth in relation to Earth's horizon line. All other planets' positions are then calculated according to their positions relative to this point.

The main advantage of this system is its accuracy when applied to modern time zones. Unlike some other house systems, it considers these changes while preserving traditional meanings associated with each house.

Additionally, many astrologers find that it gives them more accurate interpretations of individual charts than other systems.

On the other hand, there are some drawbacks to using the Placidus system. For example, it requires precise calculations based on local time zones and longitude/latitude, so it can be difficult for those without technical knowledge of astronomy or geography to accurately calculate a birth chart using this system. Also, since it relies heavily on day-specific calculations rather than night-specific calculations, some astrologers feel that critical nuances can be lost when interpreting charts, which can impact overall accuracy when assessing natal cycles or transits, for example.

# Chapter 4: Meet the Zodiac Signs

Have you ever looked up your zodiac sign and didn't have a clue what it meant? If that feels familiar, don't worry – this chapter explains the 12 zodiac signs in great detail and will help you understand their definitions and what their position means on your natal chart. In addition, it will even provide a rationale as to why it is worth learning about zodiac signs on a deeper level. No previous knowledge is needed; we are here to help anyone understand who's looking at a chart and feels completely mystified as to what it all means.

## What Are Zodiac Signs?

Zodiac signs are a set of twelve constellations that form the celestial ecliptic, or path that the Sun appears to take across the sky over the course of a year. The zodiac is divided into 12 "signs," each represented by a different symbol. Each sign has its own characteristics and qualities, and people born under these signs possess certain attributes associated with their sign. In astrological terms, each sign is ruled by a planet or two and is also associated with the elements such as *fire, earth, air,* and *water*.

The first six signs of the zodiac are

- Aries (March 21-April 19),
- Taurus (April 20-May 20),
- Gemini (May 21-June 20),
- Cancer (June 21-July 22),
- Leo (July 23-August 22) and
- Virgo (August 23-September 22)

These six signs are known as personal signs because they focus on individual traits, needs, and experiences. Aries is a cardinal fire sign represented by the ram. It's assertive, pioneering, and ambitious. Taurus is an earthy, fixed sign represented by the bull. They are known to be sturdy, practical, and stable. Gemini is an airy, mutable sign represented by twins. Individuals of this zodiac are very adaptable, communicative, and knowledgeable. Cancer is a watery cardinal sign represented by the crab and is known for being emotional, devoted, and protective. Leo is a fiery, fixed sign represented by the lion. They are known to be proud, powerful, and commanding. Finally, Virgo is an earthy, mutable sign represented by a maiden. Individuals belonging to these zodiacs are analytical, efficient, and reliable.

The last six signs of the zodiac are

- Libra (September 23-October 22),
- Scorpio (October 23-November 21),
- Sagittarius (November 22-December 21),
- Capricorn (December 22-January 19),
- Aquarius (January 20-February 18) and
- Pisces (February 19-March 20).

These last six signs are referred to as social signs because they explore relationships between individuals instead of just focusing on individual traits like personal signs do. Libra is an airy cardinal sign represented by a scale. Individuals of this group are diplomatic, fair-minded, and gracious. Scorpio is a watery fixed sign represented by a scorpion. Scorpions are passionate, resourceful but secretive. Sagittarius is a fiery mutable sign represented by a centaur. They are independent, courageous, and generous. Capricorn is an earthly cardinal sign represented by a goat. Individuals belonging to these zodiacs are disciplined, ambitious, and persistent. Aquarius is an airy fixer sign represented by a water bearer. Aquarians and known to be progressive, inventive, and rebellious. Finally, Pisces is a watery mutable sign represented by fish with compassionate, imaginative, and intuitive qualities. Now let's dive deeper, focusing on each zodiac sign individually.

Wheel of Zodiac Signs.[30]

# 1. Aries ♈

The Aries zodiac sign, represented by the symbol of a ram and its glyph of two curved horns, is the first sign in the common zodiac. Known as one of the fire signs, Aries tend to be passionate and ambitious. These traits are often reflected in their chosen pursuits or paths in life. Those in this sign have unwavering confidence and are often highly driven individuals who are not afraid to take risks or pursue something outside of the norm. This air of fearlessness is perfectly captured in their symbolic glyph, which stands for determination and stubbornness in going after what they desire. The same can be said for their symbol; just like a ram, Aries will stop at nothing to get what they want. In addition, both the symbolic glyph and animal symbol also represent leadership, much like a sheepdog would take the lead of a flock. Aries almost always takes charge when presented with a challenge or situation that needs to be handled.

Aries sign is a bold and independent sign known for its element, which is fire. Fire elements symbolize passion, adventure, enthusiasm, loyalty, and creative expression. Because of this fiery elemental quality, Aries has a cardinal modality or energy to it. This means that the people with this sign are highly motivated and take the initiative to achieve their goals. Mars is the planet that rules over Aries, and its polarity is positive because of its active character and go-getting attitude. People with this sign tend to go out and grasp what they want. They are incredibly independent, determined individuals who often have very successful business pursuits.

## 2. Taurus ♉

Taurus is one of the twelve zodiac signs and is represented by a bull. The glyph for this sign is a circle with two horns on top, depicting the head of the bull. This symbolizes strength, determination, and stability. It also represents Taurus's stubborn and hard-working nature, signifying their commitment to achieving their goals and getting things done.

The keywords that describe Taurus are: hardworking, dedicated, loyal, patient, steadfast, resilient, and reliable. They strive for stability and security in their lives and are very determined to achieve their goals. They take time to plan each step of their journey toward success and will not take any shortcuts or risks.

Taurus is an earth sign which means it values practicality over impulsive decisions or risky ventures. They prefer structure rather than spontaneity and are known for being reliable in times of need.

Taurus has a fixed modality which indicates that its energy is consistent rather than impulsive like some other signs. This helps them stay grounded when making decisions, as they don't make rash choices without considering all aspects before finally committing to something after careful thought has been given to it.

Venus is the ruler planet of Taurus which gives it qualities of beauty, love, and affection towards others, as well as acquiring material wealth through various methods such as investments or working hard at a job they truly enjoy doing. Venus also makes them artistic and creative when it comes to expressing themselves emotionally as well as by creating beautiful objects such as paintings or sculptures.

Taurus has a negative polarity, meaning that energy flows outwards into the world around them rather than inwardly towards themselves, like other positive polarity zodiac signs, for example, Aries. This gives them an outward focus where they can really channel their energies into helping others more effectively than if they were focused solely on themselves.

## 3. Gemini ♊

The Gemini zodiac sign is associated with the twins, which is represented by its glyph and symbol – two pillars or columns. It is an air sign, with the element being air, and is known as one of the mutable signs. This means that Gemini have many different facets to their personalities and are quite adaptable to various situations. They're natural communicators and tend to be very curious individuals. Their keywords are communication, knowledge, changeability, and versatility.

Gemini's air element refers to a need for intellectual stimulation for them to stay balanced. Air signs are often more analytical than emotional and strive to find logical solutions in all circumstances. They tend to value mental activities more than physical ones and like having conversations about ideas or topics that interest them.

The modality of Gemini is mutable, meaning they have an affinity towards flexibility which allows them to quickly change their opinions or beliefs when presented with new information. This also implies that Geminis can easily adapt themselves according to their environment or the people they encounter since they don't get too attached to any particular belief system due to their ever-changing nature.

Gemini is ruled by Mercury, the planet of communication, which explains why they are so talkative and witty by nature. They are always on the go and rarely rest for too long, as they crave constant activity, which keeps their minds stimulated and engaged.

Gemini has a positive polarity because it embodies transformation through communication rather than destruction through conflict, as most negative polarities do. In other words, Geminis recognize that something new can always be learned from others, even if it may contradict one's beliefs or outlook on life. This leads Geminis down a path of exploration which they approach with optimism rather than fear or disappointment because they can quickly, when needed, without worrying about any attachments.

## 4. Cancer ♋

Cancer is a sign in astrology that is represented by the glyph of a crab and its symbol of the moon. Its element is water and is associated with the cardinal modality. This means it has an active energy and an emotionally driven nature. The keywords that best describe Cancer are intuitive, nurturing, sensitive, sympathetic, and protective.

The element of water reflects the empathetic, nurturance-oriented qualities of Cancer. Water signs are guided by their feelings and sensitive to the emotional needs of others. It also represents fertility and being able to take care of oneself and others in a loving way.

Cancer has a cardinal modality that suggests an energy that focuses on creating new beginnings in one's life or environment. Those born under this sign tend to be powerful initiators who are determined to make change happen for themselves or those around them when needed.

The planet ruling Cancer is the moon, bringing out its strengths and weaknesses. The moon gives Cancer a heightened intuition, allowing them to feel connected to their inner emotions and pick up on subtle cues from others without even trying too hard. At times, however, this can also lead to moodiness and insecurity about their place in the world.

Cancer has a negative polarity meaning it is more receptive than giving but still capable of achieving great things when emotionally focused on its goals. When faced with challenging situations, they have access to deep personal reserves that allow them to stay functional despite any hardships they may face.

## 5. Leo ♌

Leo is the fifth sign of the zodiac and is represented by a lion. The glyph for Leo looks like the letter "n" which combines the sign of the sun (circle) with the symbol of a lion's mane (two crescent shapes). The lion represents power, courage, strength, and nobility – all qualities associated with this sign.

The main keywords used to describe Leo are creativity, leadership, ambition, generosity, and loyalty. This sign is ruled by the element of fire, which symbolizes passion, enthusiasm, and motivation. In other words, those born under this sign tend to be highly independent individuals that are always full of energy and ready to take on any task or challenge that comes their way.

Leo is a fixed modality, meaning its inhabitants are determined, loyal and reliable workers who stick to their plans even when things get tough. This can also mean that Leos can become overly stubborn from time to time if they feel like something isn't going as planned. The planet ruling Leo is the sun which gives these individuals strength and determination while its positive polarity allows them to shine in any area they feel passionate about.

Leos have a true heart hidden beneath their tough exterior; they are generous people who love giving back to their communities or helping out those in need. They also have great admiration for beauty, as they appreciate aesthetics more than most other signs; it's no wonder why many Leos excel in creative fields like art or music.

## 6. Virgo ♍

Virgo is one of the 12 zodiac signs spread out over a year and represents life cycles. It is a mutable earth sign, which means it has a flexible, changeable, and grounded nature. Its glyph or symbol is an M-like shape that represents femininity and the Virgin Mary, who is closely associated with this sign. This symbol is coupled with the harvest goddess Demeter who holds sheaves of wheat in her hands, representing Virgo's abundance and productivity.

The keywords that describe Virgo are: analytical, perfectionist, orderly, and practical. The element that governs Virgo is earth – which emphasizes its practicality and stability. This sign has a melancholic modality, meaning they tend to plan things carefully before taking action and can be overly critical of themselves and others. As far as planets are concerned, Mercury is the ruler of this sign, which explains why they tend to be intelligent and communicative people with great problem-solving skills.

Virgo has a negative polarity because it holds closely onto certain values and can sometimes become too critical or controlling regarding other people's ideas or creativity. Virgos need to remember that not everyone works in their own perfect way all the time. Some flexibility will help them go further in life.

## 7. Libra ♎

Libra is the seventh zodiac sign and is represented by a pair of scales, which is why its symbol is often referred to as the Scales of Justice. The Libra glyph consists of two overlapping circles with a shorter horizontal line intersecting them, representing the two sides of the scales. This sign embodies balance, harmony, justice, and fairness. It loves beauty and peace and seeks out partnerships over competition. Libra generally prefers to carefully consider both sides of an argument before making any decision or judgment.

The element associated with Libra is Air, which means it's a sign that focuses on intellectual pursuits rather than physical activities or emotions. Air signs are highly analytical and tend to be great problem solvers who can see all angles of a situation. They have open minds and communicate well with others. Air signs also have strong reasoning skills and are excellent at strategizing to achieve their goals.

Libra has the cardinal modality associated with it, meaning that this sign likes to take charge when it comes to initiating projects and leading tasks. They love taking on leadership roles because they are organized and can think things through to come up with practical solutions.

The ruling planet for Libra is Venus, which represents love, beauty, charm, and social grace. This planetary influence makes Libras people-pleasers who crave positive attention from others. They're often creative individuals who enjoy art, such as music, literature, and design.

Libra has a positive polarity because it emphasizes balance more than any other sign in the zodiac wheel. Its focus on justice makes it objective rather than subjective when dealing with matters of relationships or social interactions. People born under this sign strive for equity, whether personal or professional. They recognize how important compromise can be to keep harmony intact.

### 8. Scorpio ♏

Scorpio is the eighth of the 12 zodiac signs, and its glyph, or symbol, is represented by the scorpion. The scorpion itself can be seen as a metaphor for Scorpio's intense, passionate, and emotional nature. It suggests strength, mystery, and resourcefulness due to its defensive capabilities. This glyph reflects Scorpio's general personality traits, such as determination, power, intuition, and manipulation.

The main keywords that describe this sign are loyalty, intensity, passion, and secrecy. Scorpios tend to display strong emotions in relationships but also keep their innermost thoughts hidden from others. They often have a stoic outer shell which can be hard to penetrate. They are independent thinkers who rely on logic and fact rather than emotion when making decisions. They also make powerful allies if you can win them over with loyalty.

Scorpio is a water sign which symbolizes the element of emotion and feeling. Essentially it is all about connecting with others on a deeper level while staying true to themselves. This element allows Scorpios to be imaginative and creative and intuitively understand people around them. It allows them to express their feelings openly without fear of judgment or criticism from others, something that many other signs struggle to do.

Scorpio has a fixed modality, meaning focusing on tasks can last a long time. This tendency allows them to complete projects with great attention to detail, even if it takes longer than expected. They are also very loyal, which makes them great friends or partners. Once they commit themselves, they don't give up easily.

The planet associated with Scorpio is Pluto. In Greek mythology, he was known as Hades, which shows how mysterious yet powerful this sign can be. Pluto rules over death, transformation, rebirth, and deeper connections. These themes are all very prominent within the sign itself, as Scorpios often find themselves going through intense changes in life before emerging stronger than ever.

## 9. Sagittarius ♐

Sagittarius is the ninth sign of the zodiac and is represented by a centaur – half horse and half man -pointing an arrow up to the sky. The glyph of this sign is an archer or a bow and arrow shooting up into the sky, symbolizing ambition and aiming for higher goals, hoping to reach higher states of understanding. Sagittarius's keywords are exploration, expansion, knowledge, and abundance.

Being a fire sign, Sagittarius is all about energy, passion, action, and taking risks to reach its goals. This energy can be both creative and destructive but always with the aim of transformation. It's a mutable sign, which means it has great adaptability in terms of getting what it wants. This also means that Sagittarius can easily get bored if something doesn't challenge them enough.

The planet ruling over Sagittarius is Jupiter which gives it a positive polarity. Jupiter represents optimism, luck, and benevolence, which help Sagittarians take on any challenge without worrying too much about what could go wrong as long as they remain faithful to their beliefs. They use their expansive nature to search for learning experiences everywhere they go to gain more knowledge while having fun.

## 10. Capricorn ♑

Capricorn is the tenth sign of the zodiac, symbolized by a goat or sea goat. Its glyph is represented by a combination of the crescent moon and a fish's tail, indicating the Capricorn's dual nature as both watery and earthy. This speaks to the sign's deep desire to be on solid ground yet always open to new experiences that bring growth and change. The characteristic traits of this sign are ambition, hard work, discipline, loyalty, reliability, and a conservative approach to life.

One of the primary elements associated with Capricorn is earth, which means those born under this sign are highly grounded in material reality. They are known for their practicality and are often adept at turning concepts into tangible expressions. This makes them excellent at achieving their goals through dedicated work and persistence.

The modality attributed to Capricorn is cardinal which implies that those born under this sign are leaders who take the initiative and are naturally driven toward action. They possess great determination when it comes to attaining their objectives and overcoming obstacles along their path.

The planet associated with Capricorn is Saturn which imbues this sign with an aura of responsibility and resourcefulness. These are the qualities that allow them to achieve tangible results, even during difficult times or in the face of opposition.

Capricorns have a negative polarity as they tend to focus on themselves first before others which can lead to self-centered tendencies such as stubbornness or selfishness. However, they also use this quality as an advantage when pursuing their goals, as they know how to harness its power to avoid pitfalls.

## 11. Aquarius ♒

Aquarius is an air sign and the eleventh sign in the zodiac. The glyph for Aquarius is a stylized version of waves – and in Latin, it means "water carrier." This symbolizes Aquarius's ability to be a bearer of knowledge, ideas, and creativity, as well as its association with the element of water (which has long been associated with emotion, intuition, and mystery). The symbol also reflects the sign's rebellious nature and independence. In addition to being the bearer of knowledge, Aquarius is also known for its intelligence and unique problem-solving skills.

The keywords that describe Aquarius are innovative, unconventional, independent, progressive, humanitarian, intellectual, and idealistic. These qualities are all reflected in the sign's glyph, directly and through its connection with water (historically associated with creativity and mystery). Additionally, Aquarius is known for its capacity to think outside the box and openness to new perspectives or ways of thinking.

Aquarius has a fixed modality which means they are determined and consistent approaches to life's challenges. They have a strong sense of responsibility which helps them stay focused despite any obstacles they may face along their journey. Their fixed modality can help them stay true to their beliefs even when others around them don't agree with them or understand their point of view.

Uranus is associated with Aquarius because it represents innovation, change, and disruption – all themes that are commonly associated with Aquarians. Uranus helps to give these individuals strength when others question or oppose their beliefs or ways of thinking; it allows them to remain true to themselves without getting discouraged or giving up on their dreams.

Aquarius has a positive polarity because it values forward movement, progress, and growth. They aren't afraid to take risks or try something new rather than remain stagnant or stuck in one place. For Aquarians, it is always looking ahead toward what's next while understanding that mistakes can also be part of life's journey. This positive outlook can help encourage others around them who may already be feeling overwhelmed by life's uncertainties. It gives them hope that things will improve if they keep pushing forward, no matter how difficult things become.

## 12. Pisces ♓

Pisces is the twelfth and final sign of the zodiac. It is a water sign, symbolized by two fish swimming in opposite directions (joined by tails or a bar), representing the constant division of Pisces's attention between fantasy and reality. The glyph for Pisces looks like an "H" made from two Greek letters: iota (I) and phi (Φ). These two letters are combined to form an image of two crescent moons that represent the dual nature of the sign, its connection to both land and sea, and its ability to traverse seemingly impossible boundaries.

The keywords that describe the sign are sensitivity, creativity, adaptability, and intuition. Pisces's gentle nature allows them to be deeply empathetic towards others. They have an extensive imagination and often enjoy creative activities such as writing or painting. They are also very adaptable and can easily move between different situations without feeling overwhelmed or stressed. Pisces' intuition is renowned; they have an innate understanding of their environment and what other people need from them.

Pisces belongs to the element of water, which in astrology represents emotions, feelings, healing powers, communication, and empathy. This element gives Pisceans heightened emotional sensitivity, meaning they can feel deeply connected with people around them. It also helps them understand what lies beneath the surface of any situation quicker than other signs.

The modality associated with Pisces is mutable, meaning changeable or adaptable. This perfectly describes their ability to shift quickly between different tasks or roles when necessary. Mutability also enables them to take on multiple perspectives at once without becoming overwhelmed or confused by conflicting opinions or ideas.

Ruled by Neptune, the planet of dreams, spirituality, and illusion, this sign possesses strong spiritual convictions that give it power over its environment no matter how chaotic or unpredictable it may be at times. Its polarity is negative, meaning it reacts intuitively rather than rationally when faced with problems or challenges. It trusts its own judgment rather than relying on external sources for guidance which makes it both reliable and open-minded at times when needed most!

# Chapter 5: The Anchors and Angles of Your Birth Chart

Astrology is an art and science that can be traced back to ancient civilizations and has stood the test of time. As you know by now, the complex system of interpreting the position of the planets at the time of our birth is what we call a birth chart, and it reveals the blueprint of our life. Each birth chart has several essential points that give insights into our personality traits, emotional needs, relationship patterns, career and life purpose, and even our physical appearance. Among the many components of a birth chart, six points are considered the anchors and angles of our astrological makeup. These points are the sun sign, the moon sign, the rising sign, the DC, the MC, and the IC.

Each of these points sheds light on a specific part of our life, and they work together to create a comprehensive understanding of who we are and what we are destined to do. For example, the sun sign represents our essential self, our purpose, and the traits that define us at our core. The moon sign represents our emotional needs, our innermost desires, and how we respond to the world around us. The rising sign, also known as the ascendant, represents our outward appearance and how we project ourselves to the world. Meanwhile, the DC, or descendant, represents our relationship patterns and what we are looking for in a partner. The MC, or midheaven, represents our career path and what we are meant to do in the world. Finally, the IC, or Imum Coeli, represents our family background, our roots, and our inner emotional life.

Understanding the significance of these six anchors and angles in our birth chart is crucial in deciphering the blueprint of our life. This chapter will explore each of these points in-depth, looking at their unique attributes and how they interact with one another. Whether you're looking to gain a deeper understanding of yourself or seeking to help others navigate their life paths, the insights provided in this chapter will be invaluable. So, dive into the fascinating world of astrology and discover how the alignment of the stars at the moment of your birth shapes your destiny.

# The Sun Sign

The sun sign is perhaps the most well-known and well-understood point in astrology. It is the sign that the sun was in at the time of your birth and represents the core essence of your personality. It is the energy you radiate to the world and is the basis for your astrological identity. Each sun sign has unique characteristics and traits that can reveal a great deal about a person's character. For instance, Aries, the first sign of the zodiac, is known for its boldness, confidence, and competitive nature. On the other hand, Taurus is known for its steadfastness, loyalty, and love of comfort.

The sun sign can provide insight into your strengths, weaknesses, and natural inclinations. It can also indicate your life purpose, the areas of life in which you are most likely to excel, and the challenges that you may face. For example, the sun in Leo indicates a natural inclination towards leadership and creative pursuits, while the sun in Pisces may indicate a more intuitive and spiritually inclined nature.

One famous example of the sun sign in action is the chart of former US President Barack Obama. He has the sun in Leo, which indicates his natural charisma, leadership abilities, and creative talent. His sun is also in the 10th house, representing career and public image, indicating that his life purpose is in the public eye, where he can use his talents to make a difference.

Another example is the chart of pop star Beyoncé, who has the sun in Virgo. This indicates her precision, attention to detail, and strong work ethic. Her sun is also in the 11th house, representing community and social networks, indicating that her life purpose is to use her talents to connect with and inspire others.

The sun sign is a crucial component of any astrological reading, providing a foundation for understanding the rest of the chart. By exploring the nuances of each sun sign, you can gain a deeper understanding of yourself and others and learn to embrace your unique astrological makeup.

# The Moon Sign

The moon sign refers to the position of the moon at the exact moment of one's birth. While the sun sign represents our conscious self, the moon sign represents our emotional self and our subconscious mind. It reflects our deepest emotional needs, desires, and reactions to the world around us. The moon sign can reveal much about a person's emotional nature, instincts, and innermost feelings. It can also reveal our nurturing style and how we express our emotions to others. Understanding your moon sign can help you gain insight into your emotional patterns and tendencies and your deeper needs and fears.

Each moon sign has its own unique strengths and weaknesses that can affect how a person expresses their emotions and reacts to different situations. For example, a Cancer moon sign may be nurturing and empathetic but can also be moody and overly sensitive. A Leo moon sign may be confident and charismatic but can also be attention-seeking and egotistical. Some examples include:

Beyonce – Scorpio moon: With a Scorpio moon, Beyonce's emotional nature is intense and passionate. She is deeply intuitive and perceptive, with a strong desire for emotional intimacy and connection. She may also have a tendency towards being controlling and possessive in her relationships.

Barack Obama – Gemini moon: With a Gemini moon, Obama's emotional nature is communicative and curious. He is adaptable and versatile, with a quick wit and a love for learning. He may struggle with making decisions and may be prone to anxiety and restlessness at times.

You should remember that the moon sign can sometimes conflict with the sun sign, representing our conscious self and how we project ourselves to the world. When these two signs are in harmony, a person is likely to have a strong sense of emotional balance and self-awareness. However, when they are in conflict, a person may experience inner turmoil and emotional instability.

By exploring the strengths and weaknesses associated with your moon sign, you can better understand yourself and others. This knowledge can be particularly useful in personal and professional relationships. It can help you communicate more effectively and build deeper, more meaningful connections with those around you.

# The Rising Sign (Ascendant)

The *ascendant*, also known as the rising sign, represents how a person presents themselves to the world and how others see them. It's the sign that was rising on the horizon at the time of a person's birth, and it sets the tone for the entire birth chart. The ascendant can reveal a person's physical appearance, demeanor, and overall approach to life. It can also indicate a person's strengths and weaknesses and the challenges they may face in their personal and professional lives.

For example, a person with an Aries ascendant may be seen as confident and assertive, with a strong sense of leadership and a "take charge" attitude. However, they may also be impatient and impulsive, leading to conflict in their relationships and professional life. On the other hand, a person with a Pisces ascendant may be seen as gentle and empathetic, with a strong sense of compassion and creativity. However, they may also struggle with boundaries and assertiveness, making it difficult to stand up for themselves.

Here are two examples of famous people and their ascendant strengths and weaknesses:

Barack Obama - Leo ascendant: With a Leo ascendant, Barack Obama is known for his charisma and commanding presence. He is seen as a natural leader and has a strong sense of self-confidence. However, he may struggle with being overly concerned with his public image and may be prone to arrogance at times.

Beyonce - Virgo ascendant: With a Virgo ascendant, Beyonce is known for her attention to detail and perfectionism. She has a strong work ethic and is dedicated to her craft. However, she may struggle with being overly critical of herself and others, which can lead to self-doubt and anxiety.

By understanding your ascendant, you can gain insight into how you present yourself to the world and how others perceive you. This knowledge can be useful in personal and professional relationships. It can help you communicate more effectively and build stronger connections with those around you.

# The DC (Descendant)

The descendant, also known as DC, is the opposite point of the ascendant in the birth chart. It represents the qualities that a person seeks in their intimate relationships and partnerships. The sign on the descendant can reveal the type of partner a person is attracted to and the qualities they value in a relationship. For example, a person with a Libra descendant may seek a partner who is balanced, harmonious, and diplomatic. They may value fairness and compromise in their relationships and may be attracted to partners who have a strong sense of justice and equality.

On the other hand, a person with a Scorpio descendant may seek a partner who is intense, passionate, and deeply connected. They may value loyalty and trust in their relationships and may be attracted to strong-willed and fiercely independent partners. The descendant can also reveal the shadow side of a person's personality and the challenges they may face in relationships. For example, a person with a Cancer descendant may struggle with emotional intimacy and tend to be clingy or codependent in their relationships.

Here are two examples of famous people and their descendant qualities:

Barack Obama - Aquarius descendant: With an Aquarius descendant, Barack Obama may be attracted to partners who are independent, innovative, and socially conscious. He may value freedom and individuality in his relationships and may be drawn to partners who share his progressive values. However, he may struggle with emotional intimacy and may have a tendency to be aloof or detached in his relationships.

Beyonce - Scorpio descendant: With a Scorpio descendant, Beyonce may be attracted to partners who are intense, passionate, and deeply connected. She may value loyalty and trust in her relationships and may be drawn to partners who are strong-willed and fiercely independent. However, she may struggle with issues related to power and control in her relationships. She could also have a tendency to be possessive or jealous at times.

Understanding the qualities associated with your descendant can help you identify the partners and relationships most fulfilling for you. It can also help you to become more aware of your shadow tendencies and work on developing healthier relationship patterns.

# The MC (Midheaven)

The midheaven (MC) is another important point in the birth chart that is believed to significantly impact a person's life. The MC represents the highest point in the sky at the time of a person's birth and is associated with career, public image, and life goals. The sign and any planets that fall in the 10th house of the birth chart are used to determine the MC, which can provide insight into a person's vocational path and public persona. The MC also represents how a person wants to be seen and perceived by others and their aspirations for success and recognition.

People with a strong MC often have a clear sense of direction and purpose in their careers and are driven to achieve their goals. They may also have a strong public presence and be well-respected in their field. On the other hand, those with a weak MC may struggle to find their true calling or may lack a clear sense of direction in their career. They may also struggle with public recognition or have difficulty projecting a strong and confident public image.

As well as representing career and public image, the MC also relates to a person's reputation and societal role. The sign on the MC, as well as any planets that fall in the 10th house, can provide insight into a person's life goals and how they want to be remembered. A strong MC can indicate someone who is ambitious, goal-oriented, and driven to succeed. They may have a clear sense of their life purpose and be willing to work hard to achieve their dreams. They may also be well-regarded in their community and strongly influence those around them.

On the other hand, a weak or afflicted MC can indicate someone who struggles to find their place in the world or to make an impact on others. They may feel directionless or lack a sense of purpose and may struggle to be recognized or respected in their work field. The strength of the MC can also be influenced by other factors in the birth chart, such as the placement of the sun, moon, and other planets. Additionally, the MC can change over time as a person's priorities and goals evolve.

Here are a few examples of famous people and their MC qualities:

Oprah Winfrey – Libra MC: With a Libra MC, Oprah Winfrey is known for her sense of balance, harmony, and fairness in her career. She has built her empire on her ability to connect with people and provide a platform for diverse voices to be heard. Her public image is one of grace, elegance, and diplomacy.

Elon Musk – Gemini MC: With a Gemini MC, Elon Musk is known for his quick wit, intelligence, and versatility in his career. He has made his mark as a visionary entrepreneur known for his tech industry innovation. His public image is one of excitement, unpredictability, and brilliance.

## The IC (Imum Coeli)

The IC, or Imum Coeli, is an important point in a birth chart representing a person's family background, inner emotional life, and roots. It is located at the cusp of the 4th house, which relates to home, family, and one's private life. The IC is associated with one's earliest experiences and childhood and the emotional foundation upon which a person builds their life. It can provide insight into a person's relationship with their family, sense of security and safety, and deepest emotional needs.

In terms of family background, the sign on the IC can indicate the cultural, ethnic, or religious background of a person's family. For example, someone with a Cancer IC may come from a close-knit family with strong emotional bonds, while someone with a Scorpio IC may have a family history of intense emotions and transformational experiences. The IC can also reveal a person's inner emotional life, including their fears, hopes, and deepest desires. It can provide insight into how a person processes their emotions and how they seek to find security and comfort in their lives.

For example, Taylor Swift has her IC in the sign of Aries. Aries is a fire sign that is associated with independence, courage, and a pioneering spirit. Swift's IC in Aries suggests that she may have had a strong desire for independence from a young age and that her family dynamic may have been marked by a sense of competition or rivalry. Aries is also a sign of courage, so Swift may have had to be brave in the face of challenges or obstacles within her family.

Another example is Princess Diana, with her IC in the sign of Sagittarius. Sagittarius is a fire sign associated with travel, adventure, and a love of freedom. Diana's IC in Sagittarius suggests that she may have had a strong connection to her ancestral roots or may have felt a deep sense of wanderlust throughout her life. Sagittarius is also a sign of freedom, so Diana may have struggled to find a sense of independence within her family or may have felt constrained by royal protocol.

It's clear that the anchors and angles of a birth chart play a crucial role in shaping who we are and what we experience in life. From the fiery determination of a Leo sun to the nurturing instincts of a Cancer moon, each aspect provides a unique lens through which to view ourselves and the world around us. By gaining a deeper understanding of these key elements, we can begin to unlock the secrets of our true selves and navigate the ups and downs of life with greater insight and wisdom.

# Chapter 6: Planets, Nodes, and Asteroids

Suppose you view planets as the major players in any astrological chart. In that case, the asteroids and the nodes represent the minor players. This chapter explores both groups, describing the effects of all these entities. With a detailed introduction of glyphs, keywords, and characteristics, you'll get to delve into their symbolism. You'll learn more about their exaltation, fall, and detriment signs and what these mean. And lastly, you'll see how the energy of each planetary body affects your birth chart.

## The Major Players

The most prominent influencers on a birth chart are the sun, the moon, Mercury, Venus, Mars, Jupiter, Saturnus, Uranus, Neptune, and Pluto.

### Sun

The glyph and its role: The sun is represented by a circle with a dot in the center (☉). It indicates that the carrier of the symbol is the primary influencer over your sign and characteristics.

Keywords: Authority, brilliance, consciousness, creativity, dignity, father, gold, heart, identity, important people, king, life force, male role models, masculine energy, potential, recognition, self-expression, self-importance, sense of self, sovereignty, vitality, wellbeing.

Deities associated with the sun: Helios, Apollo, Shamash, Ra, Arev, Surya, and Ram – sun gods in different cultures

The sun is:

- Detriment in Aquarius – The least comfortable sign to rule for sun
- Exalted in Aries – The most awareness is shown in this sign
- In fall in Libra – Weakest functions in this sign

Energy summary: The sun's energy reflects in your dominant characteristics. Whichever sign the sun is in, in your birth chart, the traits of that sign will be the most strongly expressed. The Sun's energy is powerful (it's a star, after all), and so is its influence on your core personality. For example, if your sun is in Capricorn on your natal chart, your natural focus-driven, organization prone and non-nonsense traits will shine through it.

### Moon

The glyph and its role: The moon is portrayed by a crescent moon (☽) on the natal chart. It shows the reflection of your personality.

Keywords: Ancestors, belonging, comfort zone, digestion, emotional well-being and security, emotional responses, family, feelings, female role models, feminine energy, feelings, food, habits, heritage, home, instinct, maternal instincts, memories, moods, mother figures, nourishment, past, receptivity, safety, silver, stomach, unconscious responses.

Deities associated with the moon: Artemis, the Greek moon goddess, Lord Shiva, Luna, and Diana – the Roman embodiments of the moon. Selene, Khonsu, Sin, Lusin, and Chandra – moon goddesses from other cultures.

Moon glyph.[31]

The moon is:

- Detriment in Capricorn – the least comfortable sign to rule for the moon
- Exalted in Taurus – The most awareness is shown in this sign
- Is it fall in Libra – Weakest functions in this sign

Energy Summary: The moon's energy reflects the other side of your core personality. On a birth chart, it represents the power of all those traits, thoughts, and emotions you hide deep inside. However, these show who you also are (besides the characteristic of your sun sign), so don't overlook them.

## Mercury

The glyph and its role: Mercury is pictured as a circle with a cross underneath and two horns on top (☿), indicating the planet of open communication.

Keywords: Adaptability, agility, commerce, connections, coordination, eloquence, gossip, humor, information, intellect, journalism, learning, logic, messages, mental faculties, mind, nervous system, siblings, short travel, speech, thinking process, thought, transport, trickster, wits, writing, youth.

Deities associated with Mercury: Hermes, the herald of the Greek gods, and Mercury, the Roman god of communication and finances. The planet is also linked to Nabu, Lord Ganesha, Buddha, Lúc, and Thoth, deities with similar roles from other cultures.

Glyph of Mercury[22]

Mercury is:

- Detriment in Sagittarius and Pisces – the least comfortable signs to rule for Mercury
- Exalted in Virgo – The most awareness is shown in this sign
- In fall in Pisces – Weakest functions in this sign

Energy Summary: Mercury represents the energy linked to communication, intelligence, and travel. Mercury's energy affects these aspects positively, enhancing them to work better for you. When in retrograde, Mercury's energy has the opposite effect, which can cause issues.

### Venus

The glyph and its role: Venus is represented by the female symbol, which looks like a circle with a cross underneath (♀). It denotes affection and emotions.

Keywords: aesthetics, affections, arts, attractiveness, attraction, beauty, enjoyment, eroticism, female archetype, finances, glamour, grace, harmony, love, money, pleasure, relationships, seduction, self-esteem, self-worth, sensuality, sociability, throat, values.

Deities associated with Venus:

- Aphrodite, Cypris, and Venus, the Greek and Roman goddesses of beauty, love, and sensuality
- The goddesses Lakshmi, and the goddesses Inanna, Hathor, Isis, and Shukra, are all ascribed with loving, motherly, and sensual qualities

Venus is:

- Detriment in Aries and Scorpio – the least comfortable signs to rule for Venus
- Exalted in Pisces – The most awareness is shown in this sign
- In fall in Virgo – Weakest functions in this sign

Energy summary: Venus's energy is associated with love. It affects your love language, romantic side, self-love, and how you express your feelings towards yourself and others. It also has an impact on your ability to meet new people and form relationships with them – romantic or otherwise.

### Mars

The glyph and its role: Pictured as the male symbol, or a circle with a diagonal arrow pointing upwards (♂), showing direct and strong emotions.

Keywords: Action, aggression, assertiveness, blood, bravery, competition, conquest, courage, desire, drive, dynamism, energy, force, goals, heat, initiative, iron, knives, libido, lust, military, passion, physical energy, sports, sexuality, sex drive, rage, temper, virility, willpower.

Deities associated with Mars:

- Aries and Mars, the Greek and Roman war deities
- Nergal and Mangala, the Mesopotamian and Hindu deities governing war, death, and destruction

- Lord Hanuman and Anhur were two additional supreme beings linked to this planet.

Mars is:

- Detriment in Taurus and Libra – the least comfortable signs to rule for Mars
- Exalted in Capricorn – The most awareness is shown in this sign
- In fall in Cancer – Weakest functions in this sign

Energy summary: Mars's energy comes off as aggressive and typically focused on physical aspects of life. Depending on which sign Mars is in, in your birth chart, its energy can either empower you to work hard for possessions and a great physical shape (including your sex life) or leave everything to your intuition.

## Jupiter

The glyph and its role: Shown as a number four with a curved arm (♃), indicating luck and fortune.

Keywords: Abundance, aspirations, beliefs, big, chances, dogma, excess, expansion, fortune, gambling, generous, high education, hope, inflation, law, legal issues, luck, magnanimity, meaning, new horizons, optimism, philosophy, positive, religious seeker, success, travel, truth, trust, wealth, wisdom.

Deities associated with Jupiter:

- Zeus, the Greek king of gods
- Jupiter, the Roman deity of sky and thunder
- Other deities with similar roles include Lord Brahma, Marduk, the patron of Babylon, Amun, and Guru.

Jupiter is:

- Detriment in Gemini and Virgo – the least comfortable signs to rule for Jupiter
- Exalted in Cancer – The most awareness is shown in this sign
- In fall in Capricorn – Weakest functions in this sign

Energy summary: The energy of this planet is linked to optimism. Coupled with an equally optimistic sign, Jupiter can drive you to believe you can achieve everything in your life. It gives you the power to get your point across through all media and to all the right people, helping you reach your goals in all aspects of life.

## Saturn

The glyph and its role: Pictured as a curled letter "h" with a cross on top (♄), showcasing challenges and responsibilities.

Keywords: Ambition, authority figures, boundaries, career, caution, cold, conservation, conservative, destiny, discipline, duty, effort, father, fear, hierarchy, inhibition, karma, limitations, long-term planning, old age, organizations, patience, practical, prudence, reality, reliable, responsible, restrictions, rules, serious, skeleton, structure, status, tests, time, traditions, work.

Deities associated with Saturn:

- Cronus, the leader of the Greek Titans
- Saturn, the Roman god of time
- Lord Bhairav, Geb, Shani, and similar deities ruling the earth, nature, and harvest

Saturn is:

- Detriment in Cancer and Leo -the least comfortable signs to rule for Saturn
- Exalted in Libra – The most awareness is shown in this sign
- In fall in Aries – Weakest functions in this sign

Energy Summary: Under normal circumstances, Saturn's energy is associated with responsibilities. It helps you create a structured life so you can stick to all your obligations and rules. However, every 28-30 years, a phenomenon called Saturn returns, causing the planet's energies to have the opposite effects. It will emanate rebellious energies, leading you to go against the rules and structure you've followed all your life.

## Uranus

The glyph and its role: Shown as three vertical lines connected with a horizontal one, with the center line ending in a bulb (⛢), indicating originality and individualistic traits.

Keywords: Break, breakthrough, breaking rules, change, chaos, collective consciousness, detachment, eccentric, electric, electricity, experiment, extreme, fellowship, freedom, future, higher mind, impatience, independence, individual, invention, liberation, nonconformist, original, outsider, rebel, revolution, science, scientist, social, social awareness, sudden change, technology, unorthodox, unexpected.

Deities associated with it:
- Uranus and Caelus, the Greek and Roman sky gods
- Anu, the Mesopotamian king of the gods
- Nut and Aruna, deities with similar roles from other cultures

Uranus is:
- Detriment in Leo - the least comfortable sign to rule for Uranus
- Exalted in Aquarius - The most awareness is shown in this sign
- In fall in Taurus - Weakest functions in this sign

Energy Summary: The energy of Uranus is represented in your creative side. They provide power that makes you unique and express your individuality in a way only you can. For example, suppose Uranus is in Aquarius on your natal chart. In that case, it will motivate you to stand out from the crowd and go about your life following your instinct and not others.

**Neptune**

Neptune glyph.[35]

The glyph and its role: Pictured as a trident (Ψ), pointing towards creative and artistic characteristics and pursuits.

Keywords: Addiction, alcohol, anxiety, boundless, collective unconsciousness, compassion, confusion, deception, delay, delusional, disillusionment, dissolution, dreams, ecstasy, enlightenment, escapism, evasive, fantasy, fascination, forgetfulness, gas, glamour, guilt, idealism, imagination, inspiration, intangible, leaks, madness, martyr, mist, mystic, psychic, romantic, sacrifice, sensitive, spiritual, subtle, transcendence, uncertain, universal love, unknown, vision, water.

Deities associated with Neptune:

- Neptune and Poseidon, the Roman and Greek gods of water and sea
- Enki, the Sumerian water deity
- Varuna, the Hindu god of water and sky
- Khnum, the deity who created the Nile

Neptune is:

- Detriment in Virgo – the least comfortable sign to rule for Neptune
- In fall in Capricorn – Weakest functions of the sign

Energy Summary: Like Uranus, Neptune also supplies plenty of creative energy. However, Neptune's energy is channeled more towards the arts, especially for those whose Neptune is in a water sign at the time of their birth. It's particularly active in dreams and gifts you with great imagination.

## Pluto

The glyph and its role: Represented by a wine glass with a circle in the middle ( ♇ ), indicating transitional states on a birth chart.

Keywords: Abuse, corruption, crime, criminals, collective shadow, collective subconscious, compulsions, darkness, death, decay, deconstruction, destruction, elimination, empowerment, evolution, hidden, inner resources, insurance, intensity, jealous, manipulative, obsessive, pollution, power, psychoanalysis, rebirth, regeneration, renewal, repression, resentment, taboo, transformation, transmutation, underworld, violence, volcanic, wealth.

Deities associated with Pluto:

- Hades and Pluto, the Greek gods of the dead and the underworld
- Yama and Ereshkigal, Hindu and Mesopotamian deities with similar roles
- Osiris, the Egyptian fertility god

Pluto is:
- Detriment in Taurus – the least comfortable sign to rule for Pluto
- In fall in Leo – Weakest functions of the sign

Energy Summary: Pluto has a large transit time, so its energy varies greatly depending on which sign it's close to at your time of birth. It pushes forward the energy of signs it's close to. The signs that fall far from Pluto are left in the dark. However, after a transit of 30 years, this changes, allowing some zodiac signs to experience rebirth.

## The Minor Players

The Minor influencers on a birth chart are the South-North Node, the Black Lilith node, and the asteroids Chiron, Ceres, Juno, Vesta, Pallas, and Eros.

### South-North Node

The glyph and its role: Represented by half circles, with a small circle in each open end (☊ and ☋), the South-North symbol indicates a sensitive point or a precarious balance between two opposing forces.

Keywords: The connection between codependency and personal power, chaos and stability, zealotry and curiosity, masculine rigidity and feminine nurturing, cool and collected in the collective consciousness and open-hearted creativity, the undefined and the detailed, impulse and consideration, stubbornness and transformation, logic and intuition, the inner world and a concrete foundation, drama and objectivity, and rigidity and flow.

Energy Summary: The North Node's energy affects your attitude, and it can drive you toward new trends and opportunities. The energy of the South Node is reflected in innate tendencies. It results in unconscious actions and karmic patterns you'll see emerge as your life progresses. The South-North Node connection delivers a powerful force that allows you to find the balance between two opposing aspects of your life.

### Black Lilith

The glyph and its role: Represented by a dark moon with a cross underneath (⚸), this symbol points to the opposite side of the moon.

Keywords: Success, competition, winning, communication, information, influence, Worth, values, consistency, Nurture, support, sensitivities, Structure, organization, healing, Visibility, spotlight, courage,

Partnership, commitment, balance, Expansion, wisdom, exploration, Transformation, metamorphosis, depth, Determination, ambition, motivation, Intuition, psyche, creativity, Rebellion, activism, progress.

Deities associated with it: Lilith, the Great Goddess of the Earth

Energy Summary: Black Lilith energy is associated with deep-seated desires, including finding your voice and sexual liberation. It gives you the power to claim your true identity and stop hiding behind other people's actions and desires.

### Chiron

The glyph and its role: Pictured as a circle with the letter "K" attached at the top (⚷). This symbol points to wisdom and inner knowledge.

Keywords: festering wounds, source of past pain, suffering, embracing past hurts, higher purpose, the gate to spiritual awakening, learning from life experiences, hard lessons, lessons for you and others.

Deities associated with it: Chiron, a half-mortal son of Saturn

Energy Summary: Chiron's energy is a great teacher. It can show you that you'll learn far more from seeking out new experiences than from reading about them. It can also help you heal your old traumas (physical and mental) or assist others during their healing process. It teaches you that pain is only the beginning stage of healing and the best is yet to come.

### Ceres

The glyph and its role: Shown as a semi-circle with a cross attached to its bottom end (⚳), it denotes unconditional love.

Keywords: balance, seasons, cycles, attachment, disarray, conflicted emotions, being smothered, nourishment, unrequited love, unequal love, love that lays waste to everything in its path, love that leaves things to be desired.

Deities associated with it: Demeter, goddess of harvest and fertility

Energy Summary: Ceres' energy encourages you to find balance. It shows you that life is just a sequence of seasons and cycles. During each, you can form attachments and feelings – either empowering you or throwing everything into disarray. It can also show you if you're prone to let yourself be emotionally smothered or can find the balance in giving and receiving love and emotional support.

### Juno

The glyph and its role: Represented by a flower with a cross attached to its bottom part (⚛), it showcases relentless energy.

Keywords: Family dynamics, power struggle, relationships, the difference between real marriage and promises, gaslighting, entrapment, emotional blockage, demands, respect, powerlessness, answers.

Deities associated with it: Juno, the wife of Jupiter

Energy Summary: Juno's energy might indicate a place in your life where you've been gaslit. Or, you might feel trapped in a relationship power struggle. Juno's power can help set you free of emotional blockages and find answers about your relationships without risking getting hurt. It can give you the power to rule over contracts and binding arrangements you make with people in your life.

### Vesta

The glyph and its role: Pictured as a lotus flower (⚶), this symbol indicates passion, the eternal flame.

Keywords: Sexual morality, sacred places, priests, ownership over her selfhood, immaculateness, liberation and fertility, self-definition, perfectionism, uncompromising and incorruptible, a place that's meant to be yours, home as a temple, surrounding, vocation, higher self.

Deities associated with it: Vesta, the goddess of flame

Energy Summary: Vesta's energy empowers you to make your life on your own. It teaches you to view it as something sacred, something no one can taint unless you let them. And even if someone manages to do this, Vesta's energy can help you purify yourself from their negative influences and reclaim your life and power.

### Pallas

The glyph and its role: Pictured as a rhombus with a cross beneath it (⚴), it points to strengths, creative intelligence, and wisdom.

Keywords: intellect and strategy, force, sexual fire, drive, desire to conquer, a natural born leader, entitlement to rule, natural individuality, leadership, victory without compromise, born to take charge, authenticity, intensity.

Deities associated with it: Athene, a warrior queen

Energy Summary: Pallas rules over your ability to build powerful strategies toward success. She helps you incorporate wisdom, art, science, culture – or anything you feel can help you use your strategies in the best way possible. It can help you take charge of your destiny – or discover your purpose and work towards it if you haven't reached this milestone yet.

**Eros**

The glyph and its role: Represented by a heart with an arrow across it (♥), the symbol indicates one's rebellious side.

**Keywords:** courtships, romances, overexertion, power, control, inevitable trials, darkness, night, pitch black, risking everything for passion and love.

Deities associated with it: Eros or Cupid, the son of Venus

**Energy Summary:** The potent masculine energy of Eros drives you towards control. It wants you to stay on top of things, testing your faith, patience, and force of will. It makes you consider whether something is worth taking a risk for or should be left alone. It can also show you when you've been misled.

# Chapter 7: Major Planetary Aspects

Planetary aspects are another pivotal element of any natal chart since they depict an astrological interaction or a mix of planetary energies. They represent a relationship between two planets, depending on which positions they occupy relative to each other on an astrological chart. The aspects create bonds between the planets, resulting in an overall theme. For example, the relationship between certain planetary bodies on a person's birth chart can provide them with an opportunity for personal or professional growth. Other aspects create tension on the same birth chart, and a third form of aspects has complementary energy. The latter can bring you to balance the different aspects of life as they create harmony between the planetary frequencies you're affected by based on your birth chart.

You can identify planetary aspects on daily charts to see how they affect your energy on a given day. They can also help determine your astrological compatibility with people in different relationships. However, an even better way to use planetary aspects is to explore their influences on your natal chart. After understanding how they affect your personality and life, you can become more compassionate towards them and yourself. For example, you can understand how your opposition, squares, and conjunctions impact your life and how to take advantage of their effects. Empowered by this knowledge about the power of the planetary aspect, you can learn to accept yourself for who you are. It can teach you to bring out your strengths and challenge your weaknesses.

This chapter explores the meaning and role of the major planetary aspects and how they relate to birth charts. These are conjunction, sextile, square, trine, and opposition. Besides their definition and effects, you'll also read about a few examples of how they affected famous people's lives regarding manifestation and implications for each person's life.

## The Conjunction

When two planets are positioned within a couple of degrees of each other in the sky, they make a conjunction. In this position, they are usually in the same zodiac sign, which allows them to seamlessly blend their energy. It creates a perfect relationship. If two planets are in conjunction on your birth chart, their frequencies will be potent and shine intensely.

Sometimes, conjunction means new beginnings – this is usually the case if the person is born in the beginning stage of the planets' rule over their sign. For example, if you have the moon and the sun in conjunction on your natal chart, you were either born under the new moon or during a solar eclipse. Either way, the period after brings energy for a fresh start. This energy will empower you to find a connection between your conscious and unconscious desires to pursue goals that make you happy.

When two planets are conjunct, their blended energies amplify the characteristics of the sign they're in. Depending on which planets are in conjunction with which signs, the number of diverse traits that can be brought to the surface is immense. When compared to another person with a different planet conjunction in the same sign, each amplified trait can change the overall impact of that planet on a person's life. For example, suppose you have Venus in conjunction with the sun in Aries. In that case, your personality will shift towards showing your worth. On the other hand, a person who has Mars in conjunction with the sun in Aries means they are a go-getter.

While conjunctions generally impact a person's life positively, their effect depends on the planets that stand close to each other. For example, a conjunction between the luck-bringing Jupiter and relationship-based Venus will always be favorable. On the other hand, the energies of the structure-based Saturn and the passion-ruled Mars might not blend well. Still, even a challenging conjunction serves a purpose in a person's life.

They can help you learn from past mistakes, grow and offer traits that add value to your life.

Conjunctions can also be a blind spot, making distinguishing certain traits based on your natal chart challenging. For example, when Neptune is close to the sun, it can be hard to separate which planet influences a person's spiritual nature and which one affects their individuality.

There are many famous examples of people using conjunction on their birth chart to their advantage. For instance, actresses Angelina Jolie, Ingrid Bergman, Cameron Diaz, and Grace Kelly have the ascendant conjunct with Venus on their birth charts. This aspect gave them beauty and the power of attraction, which they used to gain fame and fortune.

## The Sextile

Sextiles mark a relationship between plants that are two signs apart (or 60 degrees) on the astrological wheel. Planets with ruling signs beside each other make an advantageous connection because neighboring zodiac signs have similar traits. They're usually complementary or at least don't clash in primary characteristics. For example, water and earth signs are found next to each other on the wheel. There complementary, so the planets ruling them can work harmoniously together.

Sextiles are considered one of the most positive aspects because the signs and planets involved bring out each other's positive energies. These influences affect a person's life by showing a synergistic effect. For example, if your ruling planet is Mars, whichever planet it forms a sextile with will bring out the red planet's best characteristics. They will make you action-oriented and fearless to work toward your goals and grow the strengths provided by the other planet in the sextile.

The sextile is very similar to a trine because both aspects hint at a hidden talent or something the affected person could learn or do with ease. However, there are some differences between the two. The power of the trines doesn't come naturally to people, and they serve as a reminder of one's own talents or skills. Sextiles, on the other hand, point to talents the affected person appreciates in themselves. You won't need a reminder of sextiles over because you're more likely to notice the strength they hint at and work on enhancing them.

Since sextiles involve two compatible elements, they can bring out positive vibes. Those ruled by a sextile can be sensible and happy and chilled and hard-working at the same time. This harmony blesses them with a perpetually good mood, which they maintain while jumping into action when an opportunity presents itself.

Depending on the planets involved, sextiles can be communicative and usually ready to form new relationships and camaraderie. They can direct you towards positive energies you can control and use to your advantage. They can also show you how to use your energies intelligently and intuitively. For example, suppose you have Neptune and Venus in sextile on your natal chart. In that case, you'll be gifted with a creative, romantic, almost dreamy nature. However, this depends on your ruling sign too. A person with a different ruling sign than yours can be blessed with open-heartedness and a passion for art when influenced by the same sextile.

Sextiles and trines are very similar, as they both create a unique cooperative relationship between two planets. However, the energies of sextiles will always remain separate. When they cooperate, they enhance each other's energies. They appreciate their relationship but prefer not to comingle. The power of sextile can be brought on when needed, and it takes a conscious effort on a person's part to activate these energies.

One of the most famous people with a sextile was Elvis Presley, a true cultural icon of the 20th century. He has the moon in sextile with Uranus, which granted him charisma and the ability to use his talents in music and acting.

## The Square

Moving one step further in both directions on the zodiac wheel, you'll find squares and planets divided by three signs. Since these signs are already 90 degrees apart, they are different. Their energies can clash, and quality is the only thing they share in common. However, two cardinal, mutable, or fixed signs connected by a square can bring their ruling planets into battle.

The tension created by the different energies affects their ruling planets and points. However, tension is not always a bad thing. It can motivate you to take action, even if you feel that you're ruled by forces with cross purposes. If one of the planets is more prone to landing you in a comfort zone and the other pushes you out of it, the tension between them might just be enough to make you inch your way out of complacency. It might take a while (due to being pulled into opposite directions), but eventually, you can reach your goals. That said, too much tension can lead to anxiety and stress, and it can lead you to believe that you'll never reach your goals.

Squares are often the most difficult to deal with when a person is young. These aspects will teach hard lessons, which you must learn to mature emotionally. However, until you get there, the influence of squares will be uncomfortable, conflict-prone, and incredibly challenging to bear.

Despite having the same qualities, signs involved in a square are constantly competing with each other, and the only thing you can do to deal with their influence is to compromise – just as you would when trying to please two friends who aren't seeing eye to eye. For example, suppose you have Saturn and Mars in a square in your natal chart. In that case, you'll have conflicting emotions about how to express yourself. On the one hand, you'll want to actively pursue your passions and let everyone else know about them. At the same time, you fear that you'll get criticized for wanting to pursue your dreams. This can bring incredible frustration and obstacles into your life. As challenging as this situation might seem, it will teach you how to find the best solution. You'll discover how to overcome your fear of being intimidated and confront those who might want to block your path to success. You'll learn to show them how successful you can be when using your strengths, so they'll have no choice but to acknowledge your goals.

How much encouragement you can get from a challenging square depends on the influence of the planet ruling your ascendant. For instance, if your rising sign is ruled by Venus, a square between this planet and Jupiter can be positively inspiring. However, if the square is formed with Saturn and Mars, Venus's energy will clash with them big time.

Squares can lead planets to show each other their negative sides or shadow selves. Instead of getting along, these sides will resist cooperating with each other. The more negative either planet is, or the more dominant they are in the sign, the bigger the consequence of its influence. For example, if a Saturn-ruled Capricorn is under a square between Saturn and Uranus, this will bring out all the negative influences of Saturn. However, if neither planet is particularly dominant, the Capricorn will find the much-needed balance between being true to themselves and integrity.

So, as you see, squares are demanding aspects. Still, acknowledging them can help you learn how to work with them because you can only bring light into your life if you embrace your shadows. Tim Burton is a famous example of a person with a square on their birth chart. He has Mars-square-Uranus, which granted him an uncanny ability to use innovative and unique techniques as a producer, writer, director, and artist.

# The Trine

Trines are another set of aspects that go well together. The planets forming trines are around 120 degrees apart (or four signs on the zodiac wheel). The signs are in the same element, which helps them comingle their energies. This results in plenty of good vibes, harmony, good luck, and lots of opportunities to make positive changes in your life. For example, if you have Jupiter in trine with Venus, you can have the best of both worlds. You'll carry the combined energies of the planet of luck and the planet of love - indicating that you'll be lucky in your romantic life. Trines also allow you to move forward and grow by learning from positive experiences.

However, since trines make life so easy, they can let you become too comfortable and demotivated to work for your goals. For example, suppose you have Uranus and Mercury in trine on your chart. In that case, you have the gift of open-mindedness and intelligence, and this can make it seem that you can easily do everything you want. With your positive views towards different ideas and brilliance, you'll have no trouble connecting to people and having them by your side. At the same time, because everything comes so naturally to you, this can lead you to stop pursuing new ideas.

Planets in trine support and embrace each other's energies. Because of this, if a trine rules your sign, it will inspire you to accept yourself, others, and situations. They offer you the innate talent to grow compassion and empathize with others. However, if you become too complacent, you might not appreciate the aptitudes you've been given and fail to develop them.

Fortunately, the latter rarely happens because these talents are so natural that they come almost as second nature to you. Let's say a person has Venus in trine with Neptune on their birth chart. This person will be very tolerant and accepting towards their romantic partner's personality, regardless of their differences. A person - with Venus in another aspect with Neptune - might not be able to accept their partner's differences as easily. They'll have to work much harder if they want their relationship to work.

A grand trine is made of three planets which form an equilateral triangle. On a birth chart, this means having one planetary body with different elements but still within 120 degrees of each other. This unique aspect brings even more amazing blessings because it connects the energies of three planets. Individuals with a grand trine are gifted, but the nature of their gifts depends on the planets and signs ruling them.

Unlike sextiles, trines can take each other's energies for granted. They derive power from each other in a very natural way. Their partnership is automatic, and their combined energies will flow to the person without a conscious effort to channel them on their part.

One of the most famous examples of a trine (particularly grand trine) is that of Dr. Jonas Salk, the developer of the first polio vaccine. He has a grand trine formed between Saturn, the Sun, the Moon, and Pluto. This aspect is responsible for Dr. Salk's interest in science and prompted him to get into humanitarian causes and come to a groundbreaking innovation.

## The Opposition

Oppositions are formed by planets that stand 180 degrees apart (or six signs). Because these plants govern zodiac signs that are different from each other, oppositions are challenging. Still, many people find them easier to deal with than squares. Oppositions often lead to mixed energies within a person's traits and demeanor. Depending on the plants involved, these energies can go from one extreme to another, resulting in uncomfortable situations and plenty of frustration. While this is entirely natural, oppositions also have the advantage of elemental compatibility. For example, a planet ruled by an earth sign in opposition to a planet ruled by a water sign can manage to get along. Whereas with squares, the planets involved are in non-compatible elements, making it nearly impossible for them to combine their energies. A person who learns how to make the elemental compatibility work for them can enjoy the benefits of an opposition.

Compatible elements can make the two planets in opposition fit like pieces of a puzzle, creating a balance between their union. Still, you should be aware of the obstacles to this aspect. Besides elemental compatibility, the signs also have the same quality. Their energies will rarely allow the other one to shine. These signs are set in their ways, and it takes a lot for them to make both planets work in unison. For example, if you have Pluto in opposition to Sun in your birth chart, your Pluto will be Scorpio, while your sign will be in Taurus. Due to this, you'll experiences crises in your personal life when forming relationships. While these can help you improve your life, they'll seem like major and somewhat unsurmountable obstacles at a time.

The triggered crisis can encourage you to grow, but it will take both planets to make this happen. Fortunately, people with oppositions in their natal chart tend to gravitate towards others who carry the less dominant planet in their sign. This helps them with their internal struggles as forming a relationship with those people empowers their less dominant planet. With both planets at equal strength, the opposition will bring more balance.

At the same time, people with an opposition on their birth chart can learn a lot about themselves by interacting with others. Since oppositions cause people to swing from one planet's influence to another, making you feel torn, knowing how these forces work when interacting with others can also help you balance them.

Planetary oppositions are essentially divided loyalties. They can cause inner conflict and uncertainty and make you insecure. However, unlike squares that are pressing and certain, oppositions are often wavering and uncertain. This is another reason they're more bearable. The opposition might cause discomfort in certain situations, while squares always will. You can use your opposition to balance the two opposing forces. And it only takes a little to decide which side to consider. With a square, you must be ready to become an expert negotiator and critical thinker.

Famous examples of people using opposition to their benefit are Barack Obama and Prince William. Both have the sun in opposition to the ascendant, which provided them with excellent people skills – but also great responsibilities. However, they both managed to take advantage of their talents and use them to take care of their duties.

# Chapter 8: Minor Planetary Aspects

As this chapter is an extension of the previous one, it will continue discussing the planetary aspects – only this time, the focus will be on the minor ones. Despite their name, the effects of the minor aspects aren't negligible. While they differ from the major aspects in their potency and influence, they can still help you identify significant values and meanings when interpreting your birth chart.

Like major aspects, minor ones relate to the degrees separating the participating planets in the sky. However, while major aspects explain obvious behaviors and traits, the minor planetary ones offer clues on features and occurrences that are less obvious. They relate to something people can't link to anything else.

Sometimes, minor aspects can even be more telling than the major ones. They define the meaning of planetary transit – which alters based on changes in the signs through which the planets are moving. Let's say there is a romantic relationship between a Virgo and a Libra. Both signs are ruled by the sun, enabling them to relate to each other in their own special way. Whereas another couple, an Aquarius and a Capricorn (also governed by the sun on the natal charts), might relate to each other differently. The differences between the two couples' dynamics are determined by the subtle forces of the minor aspects. Even if the aspect affecting their relationships is the same, it will affect the two relationships differently because the signs participating have different traits.

The most prominent minor planetary aspects are the sesqui-square, the semi-square, the semi-sextile, the quincunx, the quintile, the biquintile, the semi-quintile, the sentinel, and the nonile – also called *novile*. Some of these have a more powerful effect than others, but they can all provide insight into the different aspects of life when interpreting a natal chart. The minor aspects can also be valuable when analyzing charts for present situations or looking for guidance on future events or relationships.

While major aspects take on wider degrees and can have up to 10 degrees of position difference, with the minor ones, there is only a two- to three-degree orb of allowance. If the orb is more extensive, the aspects lose their potency because the planetary connections are much weaker beyond two to three degrees. As a beginner, you'll have much better chances of interpreting minor aspects of your natal chart if you stick to the planet's precise location.

Remember that the planets will not be at the same degree when interpreting minor aspects. Pay close attention to them and the signs and houses of the planets forming minor aspects. For instance, a quincunx between the sign that governs the fourth house and the sign that rules the tenth house will have slightly different effects than a quincunx between the ruler of the fifth house and the ruler of the eleventh house. In one of them, the planets will try to cancel each other's energy out. While in another one, they'll support each other.

## The Semi-Sextile

The semi-sextile is formed between two planets divided by a 30-degree angle on the zodiac wheel. The planets reside in neighboring signs with an allowed orb of one to two degrees. Because of this peripheral connection, the planets have trouble seeing eye to eye, which causes friction between them. They cover each other's energy, trying to keep each other in the shade.

In the best-case scenario, the friction between the two planets will make them attracted to each other. Their differences will make them curious about the other one's energy. This might be enough for them to put in the effort to make their relationship work. However, it will still require a lot from both to accept the other one's vibe and to incorporate it into the information they use to rule a given sign.

Neighboring zodiac signs differ because they have nothing in common – not their modality, polarity, or element. However, you can still gain something positive from a semi-sextile on a birth chart. If nothing else, you can analyze how the two planets work in tandem to see how they affect you. Once you do, you can take the steps necessary to realize the full potential they can offer you.

Despite their differences, planets in a semi-sextile have the potential to understand each other. And in most cases, understanding will happen, although it might take longer than anticipated. However, when and how the planets come to an understanding isn't guaranteed. This is why staying on top of their opposing influences is a good idea to avoid conflicts. For example, a sextile between the planets ruling Capricorn and Aquarius has unrealized potential. The two planets can highlight each other's strengths, although they prefer to focus on their differences. Yet, with a little hard work, the structure ruling Capricorn can form a strong connection with the freedom-seeking Aquarius, which the semi-sextile will highlight. There will be tension between their ruling planets, but it doesn't mean they can't make it work.

In the worst-case scenario, the aspect will only highlight the most prominent differences, leading to negative vibes only between the two planets. If the two signs can only focus on the difficulties, the planets will see any cooperation as a bad influence. Neither of them will compromise, and this will negatively impact the person affected by the aspect. They will struggle with inner conflict and might have trouble forming relationships with others, striving for total individual autonomy.

## The Quincunx

When two planets are positioned 150 degrees apart, they form a quincunx (or inconjunct). There is a three-degree orb allowance, but the closer the aspect is to the 150 degrees, the more visible its impact will be. A quincunx is another aspect that brings challenges into people's lives – as the planets involved have potent opposing forces. The influence of this aspect is much stronger than the impact of a semi-sextile. The two planets try to outcompete each other, causing irritation and friction between their energies. Suppose you have a quincunx between your ruling planet and another powerful one on your natal chart. In that case, chances are, most of your frustration in life comes from this aspect.

Just like in a semi-sextile, the sign ruled by the planets participating in the quincunx has nothing in common – so no wonder they can't come to common terms. Let's say you have a planet residing in Pisces in a quincunx with the planet governing Leo. As a passive and mutable water sign, Pisces can hardly be more different from the active and fixed fire sign that's Leo. The signs might share a few hidden traits, but their vast differences will mask this. The two approach everything in life differently. For example, a planet in Leo (fixed fire, an active sign) might form a quincunx to a planet in Pisces (mutable water, passive). Both have to do with creativity, but they approach it very differently.

The most significant impact of quincunx on a birth chart is viewed on the stress levels caused by the friction of the involved planet. The person affected by this aspect feels a constant need for adjustment. They're driven to improve something in their lives all the time. They can never be satisfied with their accomplishment, which can be stressful. Due to this aspect, some people also resort to self-soothing, which is how they overcome their dissatisfaction with life.

On the other hand, having a quincunx on your natal chart can bring you greater awareness or learning. It can help you devise a solution you couldn't think of otherwise because it teaches you to view things from different perspectives. Many believe that the two planets in a quincunx can't move forward together because they're so different that they don't know how to approach each other. This doesn't mean that their individual influences are wrong or harmful.

Due to its potential to create awareness, the quincunx is one of the most fundamental minor aspects regarding mental health. It can point to different desires you unconsciously carry throughout your life. They are hidden underneath the surface because they clash with expectations – yours and other people's. You might even be aware of some of these desires, but because you believe you'll never realize them, you keep them buried. However, you could be wrong – realizing these dreams might only be a question of trying hard enough.

The best way to work with this aspect is to become more self-aware. This will enable you to find a way to better balance the two planets' energies. Consider looking at the planets forming the aspect as two adversaries working with different tactics to reach a goal. You might even discover that they're working towards the same target. If they are, you're in luck – you only need to adjust your tactics to reach this goal.

# The Quintile

A quintile is an aspect formed by two planets set 72 degrees apart on the zodiac wheel – forming an encircled five-pointed star. There is a one to two degrees orb allowance, but beyond that, the aspect doesn't exist anymore. However, within this allowance, the aspects bring much-needed balance and harmony into the affected person's life. If you have a quintile on your birth chart, you're blessed with creative energy and the ability to maximize your talents. You're open-minded and able to see things from a perspective not everyone is able to use.

However, having all these gifts doesn't mean you won't have to work for them. The energies emanating from a quintile might be harmonic, but they will be subtle. You'll need to learn how to tap into them through your intuition. Creating something unique is all about listening to your senses and allowing your talents to flourish. By taking a proactive approach, you can cash in on your ambitions. You can create something to express yourself, but you'll also have the opportunity to impact your life and those around you.

# The Bi-Quintile

As its name implies (the prefix bi- means two), the bi-quintile comprises two quintiles. This aspect is formed between planets that sit 144 degrees apart on the zodiac wheel, with one to two degrees of orb allowance at most. Like a single quintile, a bi-quintile is also an aspect of creativity and talent. However, unlike the single quintile, a bi-quintile affects a person psychologically. If you have this aspect on your natal chart, you'll likely use your talents for pure self-expression. Material gains or making a difference in other people's lives will be on the second plan.

Still, a bi-quintile is a very positive aspect – even though its energies are even more subtle than the quintile's power. This means you'll work doubly hard to unearth those talents and skills that allow you to express yourself. Rather than waiting for the inspiration to create, you should actively engage your mind and heart to see what you can come up with. By the end, your hard work will come off – especially if one or more of the involved planets give an artistic flare to your sign. In this case, you'll have every opportunity to be as original as possible. Besides finding creative ways to express yourself, the aspect will also allow you to be inventive when finding solutions for challenging situations.

# The Semi-Quintile

Semi-quintiles are rarer than quintiles or bi-quintiles but are somewhat similar to them. They are formed by planets positioned within 36 degrees of each other (or half a quintile worth). Semi-quintiles are less potent than full quintiles, although they have the same meaning. They bring harmony and can help you make the most of your skills and talents.

Semi-quintiles provide the energy of creation, although this energy is far less persistent than in full quintiles. People with this aspect on their birth chart tend to have fewer ambitions about following their dreams. They still have a passion for creating something unique. However, this desire might be too weak for them to act on it, and it might be overshadowed by something stopping them from working toward their dreams.

# The Semi-Square

The semi-square is a minor aspect formed between planets separated by 45 degrees on the zodiac wheel, with an orb allowance of one to two degrees. As the name implies, the semi-square has half the potency of the square. This means less friction and stress, but there will be some, nonetheless. The good news is that a person with a semi-square on their natal chart won't be subjected to feeling pulled in two different directions. This leaves them with a much greater growth potential, often stunted by the stress-inducing square.

Semi-squares are associated with events and situations related to your environment. They often represent unforeseeable changes and challenging decisions you might need to make in urgent situations. If you tend to put minor issues into the back of your mind, the semi-square will happily remind you why you shouldn't do this. Heed its warnings, and the aspect will empower you to grow into the person you were destined to be based on your birth chart.

# The Sesqui-Square

A sesqui-square or sesqui-quadrate is made from one and a half square or two planets set 135 degrees apart (with a two to three-degree orb allowance). Their intensity is somewhat greater than the energy of the square – which means plenty of tension between the planets and the signs they govern.

The two planets' energies are different, forcing the affected person to choose between two energies - or learn how to use them together positively. If you have this aspect on your birth chart, you'll often be in challenging positions. Not only that, but you'll be prone to make mistakes too. It might take a few tries until you learn your lessons and overcome your challenges. Meanwhile, you'll feel like the spelling of aspects names - impossible and cranky. Because neither planet is interested in embracing the other one's energy, it takes a lot of effort not to let their differences affect you.

Instead, you should pay attention to what they have in common. These might go under the radar at first. If they do, engaging in self-reflection exercises will help you see all that's beyond the conflict. Avoid getting caught by the conflict between the two stubborn planets by focusing on what you want to do. Be honest about it, as hiding your desires will only feed into the aspects of conflicting energy.

## The Septile

A septile is formed by two planets located 51 degrees and 25 minutes apart. This egress is created by dividing the 360-degree zodiac wheel by seven - hence the name septile. This aspect is considered the source of inspiration and, depending on your sign, the creator of wonder and awe. If you have this aspect on your birth chart, you'll likely gravitate toward spiritual, artistic, or religious enlightenment. It helps you see beyond your own person, although it can help you to hone psychic talents and contribute to personal growth.

People with a septile on their birth chart often have the ability to reach into a different dimension and go beyond the mundane. Or, they at least have an open mind about spiritual experiences and strive for transformative experiences and balanced lives. If you're one of them, embrace your septile and use them to realize your dreams.

## The Nonile

Last but not least, there is the nonile, the aspect formed by two planets that are separated by 40 degrees. Noniles are made when the 360 degrees of the zodiac wheel (or natal chart) are divided by nine - hence their name. These are mystical aspects - which embrace the concept of life. They encourage a person to view themselves mystically. For example, they could prompt you to consider different endings and new beginnings in your life.

The energy of the two planets involved in a nonile is completely the opposite. If one embraces creation, the other one gravitates toward destruction. However, noniles shouldn't be viewed as a negative aspect. They teach you that even if you see an opportunity crumble in front of your eyes, another one might be waiting for you right around the corner. Life is full of possibilities, and you'll only have to choose from them when they come.

Although making a choice often makes you lose another opportunity, you'll have nothing to worry about if you've made the right decision. That said, be aware of the deceptive nature of noniles. They can make you believe that there are only two choices when, in reality, there are three, four, or even more.

# Chapter 9: Types of Chart Analysis

If you've read this book so far, congratulations on making it through the intricacies of natal chart components! By now, you have a deeper understanding of the planets, houses, and aspects and their symbolism. But how can you combine this knowledge to interpret a birth chart effectively? This is where natal chart analysis comes in. This chapter will explore the two primary methods of interpreting a natal chart – hemisphere and pattern analysis.

Hemisphere analysis involves analyzing the position of planets in the chart to determine the hemisphere in which they fall. This analysis gives you valuable insights into an individual's strengths and weaknesses. In contrast, pattern analysis, introduced by astrologer Marc Edmund Jones, identifies recurring patterns in the chart and offers a more in-depth understanding of a person's life themes and challenges.

This chapter will include a detailed description of each method and a step-by-step guideline on analyzing a birth chart using them. You'll also be provided with some easy-to-understand examples and illustrations to help you identify the most important patterns in a birth chart. With the knowledge gained from this chapter, you'll have a comprehensive toolkit for interpreting a natal chart beyond the individual components.

It's time to finally apply all your learned knowledge into action, so let's get started and explore the captivating world of natal chart interpretation through hemisphere and pattern analysis.

# Hemisphere Analysis

There are many ways to interpret a birth chart; one of the most popular methods is hemisphere analysis. Hemisphere analysis divides a birth chart into two halves, the top and the bottom, or the left and the right. This method gives astrologers insight into an individual's approach to life and their strengths and weaknesses.

The hemispheres are divided by the ascendant-descendant axis (the eastern and western horizon) or the Midheaven-Imum Coeli axis (the southern and northern hemispheres). The resulting hemispheres are then analyzed to determine an individual's personality traits, strengths, and weaknesses.

## How to Perform Hemisphere Analysis

Performing hemisphere analysis is relatively simple. First, you need to determine which hemisphere system you'll use, either the ascendant-descendant axis or the Midheaven-Imum Coeli axis. Next, you'll need to locate the dividing line between the two hemispheres on the birth chart. The ascendant-descendant system's dividing line runs horizontally across the chart, separating the top and bottom halves. The Midheaven-Imum Coeli system's dividing line runs vertically, separating the left and right halves.

Once you've found the dividing line, you can analyze each hemisphere. Start by seeing which hemisphere contains the majority of planets. Suppose there are more in the top or eastern hemisphere. In that case, it indicates an action-oriented, ambitious, and driven individual. Suppose the majority of the planets are in the bottom or western hemisphere. In that case, it shows an individual who is more relationship-oriented, passive, and receptive.

For the Midheaven-Imum Coeli system, if most of the planets are in the northern hemisphere, it indicates an individual who is more introspective, private, and focused on their inner world. Suppose the majority of the planets are in the southern hemisphere. In that case, it indicates an individual who is more extroverted, outgoing, and focused on their external environment.

## Interpretation of Hemisphere Analysis

Interpreting the results of hemisphere analysis can provide valuable insight into an individual's personality traits, strengths, and weaknesses.

Individuals with most planets in the top or eastern hemisphere tend to be more action-oriented and ambitious. They are driven to achieve their goals, take risks, and have a desire for success. They are often seen as independent and self-reliant individuals who have a strong sense of purpose and direction in life.

On the other hand, people who have a majority of planets in the bottom or western hemisphere tend to be more relationship-oriented and passive. They are more focused on their personal relationships and may be more prone to seeking approval from others. They may also be more receptive and empathetic to the needs of others, making them great communicators and team players.

For individuals who have a majority of planets in the northern hemisphere, they are more introspective and focused on their inner world. They may be more reserved and private, preferring to spend time alone or in small groups. They may also be highly intuitive and self-aware, deeply understanding their emotions and inner thoughts.

Conversely, individuals with most planets in the southern hemisphere are more extroverted and outgoing. They enjoy being around others and may be highly social and gregarious. They may also focus more on their external environment, career, or social status.

You should note that the interpretation of hemisphere analysis is not set in stone and can vary depending on the person's birth chart and other factors. For example, qualities from both sides could show up if an individual has a well-balanced chart with planets distributed relatively evenly across both hemispheres.

## Limitations of Hemisphere Analysis

While hemisphere analysis can provide valuable insight into an individual's personality traits and strengths, it's important to recognize its limitations. Hemisphere analysis is just one of many methods used in astrology, and it should not be the sole determinant of an individual's personality or life path.

Remember, an individual's personality can change over time, and while hemisphere analysis can provide insight into their current state, it may not accurately predict their future trajectory.

## Example Analysis

For this example, let's consider the birth chart of a person born on March 1, 1990, at 10:00 AM in New York City.

1. Obtain the Birth Chart

   The first step in hemisphere analysis is to obtain the individual's birth chart. This can be done using an online birth chart calculator or consulting an astrologer.

2. Divide the Chart into Hemispheres

   The next step is to divide the chart into hemispheres. To do this, draw a horizontal line across the middle of the chart, separating the top half (north) from the bottom half (south). Then draw a vertical line down the center of the chart, separating the left half (east) from the right half (west). This will divide the chart into four quadrants and two hemispheres.

3. Count the Number of Planets in Each Hemisphere

   Next, count the number of planets in each hemisphere. This example will focus on the traditional seven planets (sun, moon, Mercury, Venus, Mars, Jupiter, and Saturn). Other astronomical bodies, such as Uranus, Neptune, and Pluto, can also be considered. In the northern hemisphere are four planets: Mercury, Venus, Mars, and Jupiter. The southern hemisphere has three bodies: the sun, moon, and Saturn.

4. Determine the Dominant Hemisphere

   Based on the count of planets, we can determine that the dominant hemisphere in this chart is the northern one. Since there are more planets in the northern hemisphere than the southern hemisphere, this suggests that the person is more introspective and focused on their inner world.

5. Interpret the Hemispheres

   Once the dominant hemisphere has been determined, you can interpret its meaning. In this case, since the individual has a majority of planets in the northern hemisphere, they may be more reserved and private, preferring to spend time alone or in small groups. They may also be highly intuitive and self-aware, deeply understanding their emotions and inner thoughts.

   On the other hand, since there are still planets in the southern hemisphere, the individual may also display qualities associated with that hemisphere, such as being outgoing and social. However, these qualities may not be as pronounced as their northern hemisphere traits.

6. Consider Other Factors

   You should also note that hemisphere analysis is just one of many methods used in astrology, and it should not be the sole determinant of an individual's personality or life path. Other factors should also be considered, such as the individual's zodiac sign, planetary placements, and aspects between planets.

   For example, suppose the individual has a dominant planet that is located in the southern hemisphere. In that case, this may counteract some of the northern hemisphere's qualities. Additionally, the individual's rising sign (also known as the ascendant) can significantly impact their personality traits.

Overall, hemisphere analysis can be useful in astrology for gaining insight into a person's approach to life and development. By analyzing the distribution of planets across hemispheres, astrologers can identify patterns and tendencies that can be used to better understand an individual's personality.

## Pattern Analysis

Pattern analysis is another powerful method in astrology to gain insight into an individual's personality and life path. By analyzing the distribution and interplay of the planets and other astronomical bodies in a birth chart, astrologers can identify patterns and tendencies that can provide valuable information about an individual's character, strengths, and weaknesses.

Pattern analysis involves examining a birth chart's overall shape and structure to identify patterns and themes that can provide insight into an individual's personality and life path. Astrologers look for patterns such as stelliums (groupings of planets in a single sign or house), planetary patterns (such as grand trines or T-squares), and dominant planets or elements.

The goal of pattern analysis is to identify the underlying patterns and themes that shape an individual's life and to use this information to help the individual gain a deeper understanding of themselves and their potential.

### Types of Patterns

Astrologers may look for many different types of patterns in a birth chart. Here are a few of the most common:

1. **Stelliums:** A stellium is a grouping of three or more planets in a single sign or house. Stelliums are considered significant because they can indicate a concentration of energy and activity in a particular area of life. For example, an individual with a stellium in the seventh house (the house of partnerships) may strongly focus on relationships and partnerships throughout their life.

2. **Grand Trines:** A grand trine is a pattern formed by three planets evenly spaced around the chart, forming an equilateral triangle. Grand trines are considered significant because they indicate a harmonious flow of energy and talent in a particular area of life. For example, an individual with a grand trine in the earth signs (Taurus, Virgo, and Capricorn) may have a natural talent for practical, material, and financial matters.

3. **T-Squares:** A T-square is a pattern formed by three planets in a square (90-degree) aspect to each other, with one planet opposing the other two. T-squares are considered significant because they can indicate tension or challenge in a particular area of life. For example, an individual with a T-square involving the sun, moon, and Saturn may struggle with self-expression, emotional fulfillment, and authority or responsibility issues.

4. **Dominant Planets or Elements:** Astrologers may also look at the distribution of planets or elements (fire, earth, air, and water) in a chart to identify dominant influences. For example, an individual with a dominant Saturn may have a strong sense of responsibility and discipline, while an individual with a dominant water element may be highly emotional and intuitive.

### Interpreting Patterns

Once an astrologer has identified patterns in a birth chart, the next step is interpreting their meaning. This involves considering the individual's zodiac sign, planetary placements, aspects between planets, and the specific patterns that have been identified.

For example, suppose an individual has a stellium in the 10th house (the house of career and public image). In that case, the astrologer may interpret this as indicating a strong focus on career and achievement throughout the individual's life. The specific planets involved in the stellium and any aspects between them and other planets in the chart can provide additional information about the individual's talents, strengths, and potential challenges.

Similarly, suppose an individual has a T-square involving the moon, Uranus, and Pluto. In that case, the astrologer may interpret this as indicating a tension or challenge related to emotional expression, freedom, and transformation. The specific signs and houses involved in the T-square and any aspects between the planets and other astronomical bodies in the chart can provide additional information about the nature of the challenge and potential strategies for resolving it.

### Examples of Pattern Analysis

To illustrate how pattern analysis works in practice, let's consider a few examples:

### Example 1: Stellium in the 2nd House

Imagine that an individual has a stellium of planets (sun, moon, Venus, and Mars) in the second house of their birth chart, which governs finances, possessions, and values. This could indicate a strong focus on financial matters and material possessions throughout the individual's life. The specific planets involved in the stellium can provide additional insight:

- **Sun:** The sun represents the core of one's personality and sense of self. With the sun in the second house, this person may have a strong sense of self-worth and a desire for financial stability.
- **Moon:** The moon represents one's emotions and inner world. With the Moon in the second house, this individual may find emotional security in their material possessions and financial situation.
- **Venus:** Venus represents one's values and relationships. With Venus in the second house, this individual may place a high value on material possessions and financial stability and may seek out relationships that provide them with a sense of financial security.
- **Mars:** Mars represents one's energy and drive. With Mars in the second house, this individual may be highly motivated to achieve financial success and may be willing to work hard to achieve their financial goals.

Overall, this stellium in the second house could indicate a strong focus on financial matters and material possessions throughout this individual's life, particularly emphasizing building financial security and stability.

**Example 2: Grand Trine in the Water Signs**

Imagine that an individual has a grand trine of planets (Jupiter, Neptune, and Pluto) in the water signs (Cancer, Scorpio, and Pisces), which govern emotions, intuition, and creativity. This could indicate a strong emotional and creative energy flow throughout the individual's life. The specific planets involved in the grand trine can provide additional insight:

- **Jupiter:** Jupiter represents expansion and growth. With Jupiter in a water sign, this individual may experience emotional growth and expansion throughout their life and may have a strong intuition and connection to the subconscious.
- **Neptune:** Neptune represents dreams, imagination, and spirituality. With Neptune in a water sign, this individual may be highly creative and intuitive, with a deep connection to their dreams and inner world.
- **Pluto:** Pluto represents transformation and regeneration. With Pluto in a water sign, this individual may experience deep emotional transformations throughout their life and may have a strong intuition for navigating complex emotional situations.

Overall, this grand trine in the water signs would indicate a strong flow of emotional and creative energy throughout this individual's life, particularly emphasizing emotional growth, imagination, and transformation.

Astrology offers a rich and complex framework for understanding the unique and multifaceted nature of human personality and experience. Using different chart analysis techniques like hemisphere analysis, and pattern analysis, you get valuable insights into an individual's strengths, challenges, and life path. By weaving together these different analysis threads, you can paint a vivid and nuanced portrait of an individual's birth chart, offering guidance and support for personal growth and development. In a world where self-discovery is an ongoing journey, astrology is a valuable tool for exploring the depths of our inner world and unlocking the mysteries of our place in the universe.

# Chapter 10: How to Read Any Chart

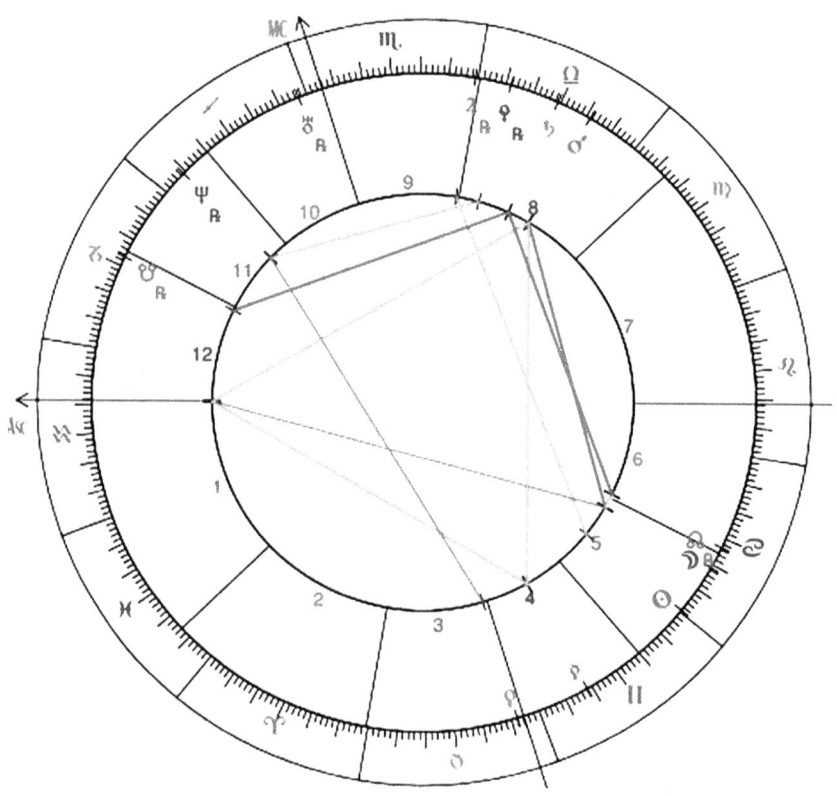

Sample birth chart with elements.[24]

Welcome to the grand finale of this astrological journey! You now have a solid foundation of the building blocks of astrology: the planets, the signs, the houses, and the aspects. You've learned how to construct and read a birth chart and explored different types of chart analysis, from the hemispheric approach to the pattern analysis method.

Now, it's time to put all that knowledge into practice and learn how to interpret any chart confidently and easily. In this final chapter, you will be provided with a step-by-step guide on how to read any birth chart, whether it's your own or someone else's. It will take you through the process of collecting and analyzing chart elements, identifying patterns and configurations, and synthesizing the information to create a comprehensive interpretation of the chart.

The best way to apply your learned knowledge is to put it into action, and that's exactly what you'll get to do in this chapter. You will be given several example birth charts and the step by step instructions to interpret them. By the end of this chapter, you'll have all the tools you need to read any birth chart with confidence and accuracy. So, get ready to put your astrological skills to the test!

## Step-by-Step Guide to Interpreting Any Chart

Interpreting a birth chart may seem daunting at first, but with the right approach, it can be a fulfilling and enlightening experience. Here is a step-by-step guide to help get you started:

1. Collecting Information

    Before analyzing the chart, you need to gather all your information. This includes the individual's birth data, including their birth date, time, and location. Once you have this information, you can use it to create a birth chart by drawing a wheel that represents the position of the planets at the time of birth.

2. Examining the Chart Elements

    The planets, houses, signs, and aspects are the key elements of a birth chart. To interpret the chart, you need to understand each of these elements and how they relate to one another.

    Firstly, observe the position of each planet in the chart, noting the sign and house it is located in. Understanding the meaning of each planet and how it represents different aspects of an individual's personality and life experiences is crucial. Then, examine the planetary aspects, which are the angles between the planets, and note any major or minor aspects that stand out.

Analyzing the houses in which the planets are located is also necessary, and understanding the meaning of each house and how it relates to different areas of life is vital. It is also necessary to know the ruler of each house, which is the planet that rules over the sign of the house cusp, and note its position and aspects.

Afterward, consideration of the signs that the planets are in and how they influence the planet's expression is necessary. Finally, taking note of the elements and modes of the signs, which give insight into the individual's temperament and approach to life, completes the process.

3. Analyzing the Chart

Once you understand the chart elements well, you can start analyzing the chart. The first step is identifying patterns or configurations in the chart, such as stelliums or grand trines. These patterns give you additional information about the individual's personality and life path.

Next, you should examine the planetary aspects, both major and minor, and consider the relationships between the planets. Rulerships, dispositor chains, and mutual receptions are all useful tools for understanding these relationships.

4. Synthesizing the Information

The final step in interpreting a birth chart is to bring all the information together and synthesize it into a comprehensive interpretation. This involves identifying themes and patterns in the chart and interpreting the chart as a whole.

Following these steps, you can interpret any birth chart confidently and accurately. Remember, interpreting a birth chart is a lifelong process, and the more you practice, the better you will understand astrology's complexities.

# Example Interpretations

**Bradley Cooper**

Let's take the example birth chart of actor and director Bradley Cooper, born on January 5th, 1975, at 5:38 am in Philadelphia, Pennsylvania.

1. **Collecting Information**

    Before interpreting Cooper's birth chart, you must gather basic information about his birth. This includes his birth date, time, and location. Once this information has been obtained, his birth chart can be generated using astrology software, an online birth chart calculator, or even drawn up by hand.

2. **Examining the Chart Elements**

    **The Planets**

    Once Cooper's birth chart is drawn up, the interpretation process can begin; this starts with examining various elements within it. First, you need to look at the positions of the planets. Cooper's chart includes the following planets:

    - Sun in Capricorn
    - Moon in Libra
    - Mercury in Sagittarius
    - Venus in Aquarius
    - Mars in Sagittarius
    - Jupiter in Pisces
    - Saturn in Cancer
    - Uranus in Scorpio
    - Neptune in Sagittarius
    - Pluto in Libra

    **The Houses**

    Next, look at the houses in Cooper's birth chart. Each house represents a different area of life, and the sign that rules each house gives us additional information about how that area of life is expressed. Cooper's houses are as follows:

    - First House: Self, identity, appearance – ruled by Capricorn

- Second House: Money, possessions, values – ruled by Aquarius
- Third House: Communication, siblings, short trips – ruled by Pisces
- Fourth House: Home, family, roots – ruled by Aries
- Fifth House: Creativity, children, romance – ruled by Taurus
- Sixth House: Health, work, service – ruled by Gemini
- Seventh House: Relationships, partnerships – ruled by Cancer
- Eighth House: Intimacy, shared resources – ruled by Leo
- Ninth House: Philosophy, travel, education – ruled by Virgo
- Tenth House: Career, reputation, public image – ruled by Libra
- Eleventh House: Friendships, groups, social causes – ruled by Scorpio
- Twelfth House: Secrets, spirituality, subconscious – ruled by Sagittarius

## 3. Analyzing the Chart

### Identifying Patterns

Once you've examined Cooper's chart's individual elements, you can look for patterns and connections between them. One notable pattern in Cooper's chart is the stellium (a grouping of three or more planets in one sign or house) in Sagittarius, which includes Mercury, Mars, and Neptune.

### Examining the Aspects

You also need to examine the aspects between the planets – the geometric angles formed between them. Cooper's chart includes several major aspects, including:

- Sun square Jupiter
- Moon trine Venus
- Mercury conjunct Mars
- Venus square Mars
- Jupiter conjunct Neptune

- Saturn trine Neptune
- Uranus sextile Pluto

### Considering Planetary Relationships

You can also examine the relationships between the planets by looking at rulerships, dispositor chains, and mutual receptions. In Cooper's chart, Jupiter is the ruler of both Pisces (which rules his third house) and Sagittarius (which rules his stellium). Neptune is the dispositor of his stellium in Sagittarius and is also conjunct with Jupiter in Pisces.

## 4. Synthesizing the Information

### Bringing Together the Different Chart Elements

Now that you've examined the individual elements of Cooper's chart and identified patterns and connections between them, you can begin to synthesize the information to gain a deeper understanding of his character and potential life path. One key theme that emerges is Cooper's strong emphasis on creativity, as seen in his stellium in the fifth house and the presence of Neptune in the first house. This suggests that artistic pursuits may significantly affect his life and career.

Another theme is Cooper's potential for leadership and ambition, as indicated by his Mars in the 10th house and Saturn in the first house. This combination could suggest a strong drive for success and a disciplined approach to achieving his goals.

### Identifying Themes and Patterns

Combining the different chart elements and considering their interactions allows you to identify some overall themes and patterns in Cooper's chart. One possible interpretation is that he has a strong sense of purpose and a drive to succeed, which may be expressed through his artistic pursuits or other areas of his life. At the same time, Cooper may also struggle with balancing his personal goals with his relationships and emotional needs, as indicated by his T-square involving Venus, Pluto, and Uranus.

### Interpreting the Chart as a Whole

When interpreting a birth chart, keep in mind that each element is connected to others and contributes to a larger whole. In Cooper's case, you can see a complex interplay between creativity, ambition, and emotional depth, which may manifest in various ways throughout his life.

Overall, his chart suggests a driven, creative, and ambitious person with the potential for leadership and success in his chosen field. However, he may also face challenges in balancing his personal and professional goals and navigating complex emotional dynamics in his relationships.

## Selena Gomez

Let's take another example here. Singer Selena Gomez was born on July 22, 1992, at 6:35 am in Grand Prairie, Texas.

### 1. Collecting Information

Before interpreting Gomez's birth chart, we need to gather basic information about her birth, including her birth date, time, and location. Once this information is obtained, we can generate her birth chart using astrology software or an online calculator.

### 2. Examining the Chart Elements

#### The Planets

Gomez's birth chart includes the following planets:
- Sun in Cancer
- Moon in Aries
- Mercury in Cancer
- Venus in Leo
- Mars in Taurus
- Jupiter in Virgo
- Saturn in Aquarius
- Uranus in Capricorn
- Neptune in Capricorn
- Pluto in Scorpio

#### The Houses

Next, we need to observe the houses in Gomez's birth chart. Her houses are as follows:
- First House: Self, identity, appearance – ruled by Cancer
- Second House: Money, possessions, values – ruled by Leo
- Third House: Communication, siblings, short trips – ruled by Virgo

- Fourth House: Home, family, roots – ruled by Libra
- Fifth House: Creativity, children, romance – ruled by Scorpio
- Sixth House: Health, work, service – ruled by Sagittarius
- Seventh House: Relationships, partnerships – ruled by Capricorn
- Eights House: Intimacy, shared resources – ruled by Aquarius
- Ninth House: Philosophy, travel, education – ruled by Pisces
- Tenth House: Career, reputation, public image – ruled by Aries
- Eleventh House: Friendships, groups, social causes – ruled by Taurus
- Twelfth House: Secrets, spirituality, subconscious – ruled by Gemini

## 3. Analyzing the Chart
### Identifying Patterns

One notable pattern in Gomez's chart is the T-square involving her moon in Aries, Pluto in Scorpio, and Uranus in Capricorn. This aspect pattern indicates potential tension and conflict in the areas of relationships and emotional expression. Additionally, Gomez has a grand trine involving her sun in Cancer, Saturn in Aquarius, and Neptune in Capricorn, suggesting a harmonious and creative energy.

### Examining the Aspects

Gomez's chart includes several major aspects, including:
- Sun trine Jupiter
- Moon square Pluto
- Mercury trine Neptune
- Venus square Uranus
- Jupiter sextile Uranus
- Saturn trine Neptune
- Uranus sextile Neptune

### Considering Planetary Relationships

In Gomez's chart, Jupiter is the ruler of her Sagittarius Midheaven, indicating potential success and growth in her career. Additionally, Uranus and Neptune are in mutual reception, suggesting a connection between her ability to express herself creatively (Neptune) and her desire for individuality and freedom (Uranus).

## 4. Synthesizing the Information

### Bringing Together the Different Chart Elements

By examining the individual elements of Gomez's chart and identifying patterns and connections between them, we can synthesize the information and better understand her character and potential life path. One key theme that emerges is Gomez's potential for emotional intensity and transformation, as indicated by her T-square involving the moon, Pluto, and Uranus. This may manifest in her personal relationships, as well as in her creative and professional pursuits.

Another theme is Gomez's potential for success and growth in her career, indicated by the grand trine involving her sun, Saturn, and Neptune. This suggests that she may have a strong work ethic and a creative talent that could lead to long-term success and recognition.

### Identifying Themes and Patterns

Overall, Gomez's chart suggests a highly intuitive, sensitive, and empathic person with a deep connection to her emotions and inner world. Her strong emphasis on water signs (Cancer, Scorpio, and Pisces) and the moon in her first house suggests that her emotional needs and inner life are central to her identity and how she relates to the world around her.

Another theme in Gomez's chart is her potential for creativity and self-expression, as seen in her stellium in the fifth house, which includes Mercury, Venus, and Jupiter. This suggests that artistic pursuits may be an important part of her life and may play a significant role in her career.

In addition, Gomez's chart indicates a strong drive for independence and a desire to assert herself, as seen in her Mars in Aries in the eighth house. This placement suggests that she may be a natural leader with a talent for mobilizing others around a cause or project.

### Interpreting the Chart as a Whole

When interpreting Gomez's birth chart, it's essential to consider the interplay between the elements and how they contribute to her character and potential life path. Her chart suggests a person deeply connected to her emotions and inner world, with a talent for creativity and self-expression. However, she may also struggle with issues of independence and self-assertion, particularly in the context of relationships and partnerships.

Overall, Gomez's chart suggests a complex and dynamic personality with the potential for significant achievements in both artistic and personal realms. As with any birth chart interpretation, it's important to remember that the chart provides a map of potentials rather than a predetermined destiny and that individuals always have the power to make choices and shape their lives in meaningful ways.

## Additional Tips for Chart Interpretation

Several factors must be considered when interpreting a chart to ensure a thorough and accurate analysis. Firstly, look at the chart as a whole and consider how different elements interact with each other. For example, a strong placement of Jupiter in the tenth house may indicate a person with a high potential for success in their career, but if that placement is squared by Saturn in the first house, there may be challenges or obstacles that need to be overcome. It's also important to consider the strength of the planets and houses in the chart and any major aspects or patterns.

Another factor to consider is each planet's astrological sign and element, as well as any placements in specific degrees or decans. This can give additional insight into a person's personality, tendencies, and potential challenges. For example, a person who has a strong emphasis on the sign of Scorpio may have intense emotions and a deep desire for transformation, while a person with several planets in the air signs may be highly analytical and cerebral.

One must be aware of potential challenges and pitfalls when interpreting a chart. One common mistake is to focus too much on the positive placements and overlook potential challenges or negative aspects. Also, avoid stereotyping or making assumptions based on a person's chart, as everyone is unique and complex.

Finally, using intuition and personal experience when interpreting a chart is important. While general guidelines and interpretations exist for each element, each chart is unique and may require a more nuanced approach. You should also consider the person's individual experiences and circumstances, as well as their own intuition and insights.

Interpreting a birth chart can be a complex but rewarding process. By understanding the basic components of a chart and the various factors that can influence its interpretation, you can gain valuable insights into yourself and others. Remember to approach chart interpretation with an open mind, considering both objective data and your own intuition and personal experience. With practice and patience, you can become adept at reading birth charts and using this knowledge to deepen your understanding of yourself and the world around you.

# Glossary of Glyphs

The glyphs and symbols for all planets and signs each have a meaning behind them. Here is a list of the abbreviations used for some of the most common terms in astrology:

MC - Midheaven (also called Medium Coeli): This is the highest point at any given time in an individual's chart, representing ambition, career goals, and personal destiny.

ASC - Ascendant (also called Rising Sign): This is the sign that was rising on the horizon at the exact moment of birth, representing physical characteristics, public persona, and how we appear to others.

DSC - Descendant (also called Setting Sign): This is the opposite of the ascendant and represents relationships, marriage, and partnerships.

# Houses

1. First House (Ascendant): Represents the self, physical body, and personality; symbolized by the ram;
2. Second House: Represents material values, money, and possessions; symbolized by the bull;
3. Third House: Represents communication, education, and intellectual pursuits; symbolized by two fish swimming in opposite directions;
4. Fourth House: Represents family matters, home environment, and personal roots; symbolized by a crab walking sideways;
5. Fifth House: Represents creativity, romance, and children/pregnancy; symbolized by a Lion;
6. Sixth House: Represents work and service, health and hygiene; symbolized by a virgin holding a sheaf of wheat;
7. Seventh House: Represents partnerships, marriage, and public relationships; symbolized by two scales balancing each other out;
8. Eighth House: Represents death and transformation, joint finances and investments; symbolized by an eagle with its wings spread wide open;
9. Ninth House: Represents higher learning, philosophy, exploration, and travel/relocation; symbolized by the archer aiming an arrow towards the sky;
10. Tenth House: Represents career, public life, ambition, and authority; symbolized by a bull carrying a horn of plenty;
11. Eleventh House: Represents hopes and wishes, friendships and associations; symbolized by an Aquarius pouring out water from two jugs;
12. Twelfth House: Represents secrets, sorrows, and subconscious patterns; symbolized by a mermaid or manatee in the depths of the sea;

# Planets

Sun: ♂ - This symbol represents the masculine energy associated with the sun, which is related to power, authority, identity, and ambition.

Moon: ♀ - This symbol represents the feminine energy associated with the moon, which is related to emotions, intuition, and feelings.

Mercury: ☿ - This symbol represents communication, intellect, and logic. It is also associated with writing, speaking, and traveling.

Venus: ♀ - This symbol represents love, beauty, relationships, and all things that bring joy and pleasure into our lives. It can also be seen as a representation of our values.

Mars: ♂ - This symbol represents passion, energy, and aggression. It is associated with ambition, drive, courage, and determination.

Jupiter: ♃ - This symbol represents expansion, abundance, and luck. It is related to higher education, new opportunities, and growth.

Saturn: ♄ - This symbol represents structure, boundaries, and discipline. It is associated with responsibility, hard work, and obligations in life.

Uranus: ♅ - This symbol represents independence, freedom, and innovation. It is related to creativity and unexpected changes that can happen suddenly in our lives.

Neptune: ♆ - This symbol represents dreams, illusions, and spirituality. It is associated with imagination, empathy, compassion, and faith.

Pluto: ♇ - This symbol represents transformation, rebirth, and power. It is related to death and renewal as well as secrets and hidden truths in life.

Chiron- Chiron is an asteroid that is often referred to as a "centaur" because it orbits between the orbits of Saturn and Uranus and is considered to have both planetary energy and comet-like energy. It has been nicknamed "the wounded healer" due to its association with healing from wounds and pain, both emotional and physical. Abbreviation: Chi

# Zodiac Signs

Symbol: ♈ Aries - Abbreviation: Ari

Meaning: This symbol represents the sign of Aries, which is represented by a ram. It symbolizes leadership, courage, passion, and creativity.

Symbol: ♉ Taurus - Abbreviation: Tau

Meaning: This symbol represents the sign of Taurus, which is represented by a bull. It symbolizes strength, stability, dependability, and perseverance.

Symbol: ♊ Gemini - Abbreviation: Gem

Meaning: This symbol represents the sign of Gemini, which is represented by two twins. It symbolizes communication, adaptability, intelligence, and versatility.

Symbol: ♋ Cancer - Abbreviation: Can

Meaning: This symbol represents the sign of Cancer, which is represented by a crab. It symbolizes emotions, sensitivity, intuition, and nurturing.

Symbol: ♌ Leo- Abbreviation: Leo

Meaning: This symbol represents the sign of Leo, which is represented by a lion. It symbolizes strength, confidence, and vitality.

Symbol: ♍ Virgo - Abbreviation: Vir

Meaning: This symbol represents the sign of Virgo, which is represented by a maiden. It symbolizes intelligence, detail-orientedness, and practicality.

Symbol: ♎ Libra - Abbreviation: Lib

Meaning: This symbol represents the sign of Libra, which is represented by a set of scales. It symbolizes balance, fairness, and diplomacy.

Symbol: ♏ Scorpio - Abbreviation: Sco

Meaning: This symbol represents the sign of Scorpio, which is represented by a scorpion. It symbolizes passion, intensity, and power.

Symbol: ♐ Sagittarius - Abbreviation: Sgr

Meaning: This symbol represents the sign of Sagittarius, which is represented by an archer. It symbolizes optimism, adventure, and ambition.

Symbol: ♑ Capricorn - Abbreviation: Cap

Meaning: This symbol represents the sign of Capricorn, which is represented by a goat. It symbolizes hard work, discipline, and ambition.

Symbol: ♒ Aquarius - Abbreviation: Aqr

Meaning: This symbol represents the sign of Aquarius, which is represented by a wave. It symbolizes creativity, inventiveness, and humanitarianism.

Symbol: ♓ Pisces - Abbreviation: Psc

Meaning: This symbol represents the sign of Pisces, which is represented by two fish swimming in opposite directions. It symbolizes empathy, compassion, and sensitivity.

These symbols have been used for centuries to represent the different astrological signs and planets. They are universal representations of the specific traits associated with each one and can provide insight into a person's character and personality. Understanding these symbols is essential for an accurate assessment of an individual's astrological chart, as well as to gain a better understanding of how the universe affects us all.

Sextile: A sextile is an astrological aspect formed when two planets are 60 degrees apart. This symbol is represented by a circle containing a plus sign. The abbreviation for this aspect is SXT.

Conjunction: A conjunction is an astrological aspect formed when two planets are within eight to ten degrees of each other. This symbol is represented with a circle containing an equals sign, and the abbreviation for this aspect is Cnj.

Trine: A trine is an astrological aspect formed when two planets are 120 degrees apart. This symbol is represented by a triangle, and the abbreviation for this aspect is Trn or Tri.

Square: A square is an astrological aspect formed when two planets are 90 degrees apart. This symbol is represented with a square, and the abbreviation for this aspect is Sqr.

Opposition: An opposition is an astrological aspect formed when two planets are 180 degrees apart. This symbol is represented by a circle containing a diagonal line, and the abbreviation for this aspect is Opp.

Quincunx: A quincunx is an astrological aspect formed when two planets are 150 degrees apart. This symbol is represented by a circle containing five dots, and the abbreviation for this aspect is Qcn or Quin.

Semi-square: A semi-square (or semisquare) is an astrological aspect formed when two planets are 45 degrees apart. This symbol is represented by a circle containing four dots, and the abbreviation for this aspect is SSq or Ssq.

Sesquiquadrate: A sesquiquadrate (or sesqui-quadrates) is an astrological aspect formed when two planets are 135 degrees apart. This symbol is represented by a circle containing six dots, and the abbreviation for this aspect is SQQ or Squa.

Semisextile: A semisextile (or semi-sextiles) is an astrological aspect formed when two planets are 30 degrees apart. This symbol is represented by a circle containing three dots, and the abbreviation for this aspect is SSx or Ssx.

Quintile: A quintile (or quincunxes) is an astrological aspect formed when two planets are 72 degrees apart. This symbol is represented by a circle containing five lines radiating outward from a point in the center, and the abbreviation for this aspect is Qui.

Septile: A septile (or septiles) is an astrological aspect formed when two planets are 51 degrees 20 minutes apart. This symbol is represented by a circle containing seven lines radiating outward from a point in the center, and the abbreviation for this aspect is Sep.

Novile: A novile (or noviles) is an astrological aspect formed when two planets are 40 degrees apart. This symbol is represented by a circle containing nine lines radiating outward from a point in the center, and the abbreviation for this aspect is Nov.

Binovile: A binovile (or binoviles) is an astrological aspect formed when two planets are 20 degrees apart. This symbol is represented by a circle containing two points connected by two lines radiating outward from another point in the center, and the abbreviation for this aspect is BNv.

Decile: A decile (or decilions) is an astrological aspect formed when two planets are 36 degrees apart. This symbol is represented by a circle containing ten lines radiating outward from a point in the center, and the abbreviation for this aspect is Dcl.

# Bonus: Birth Chart Templates

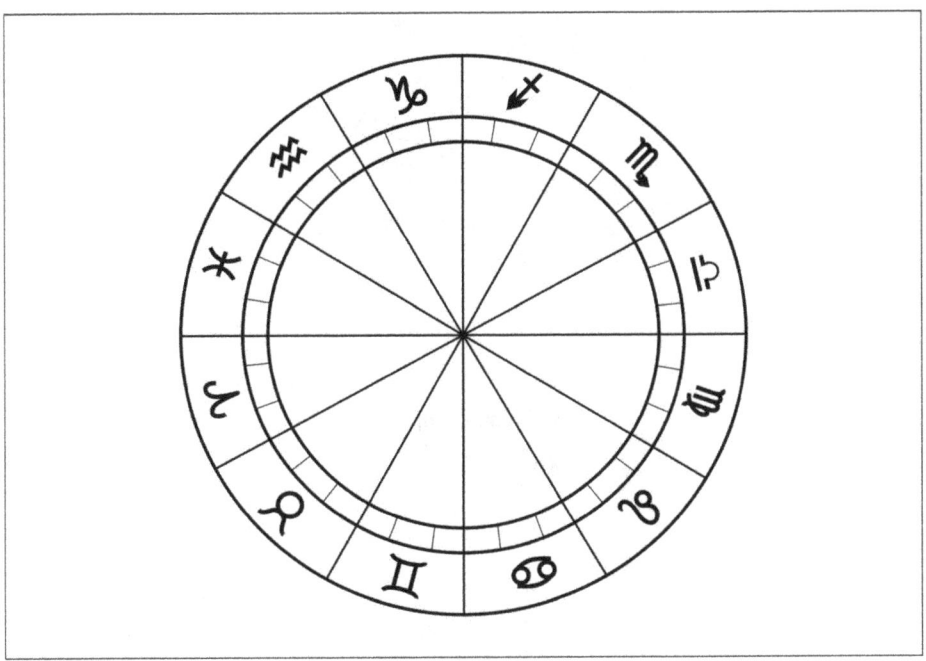

Birth chart template.

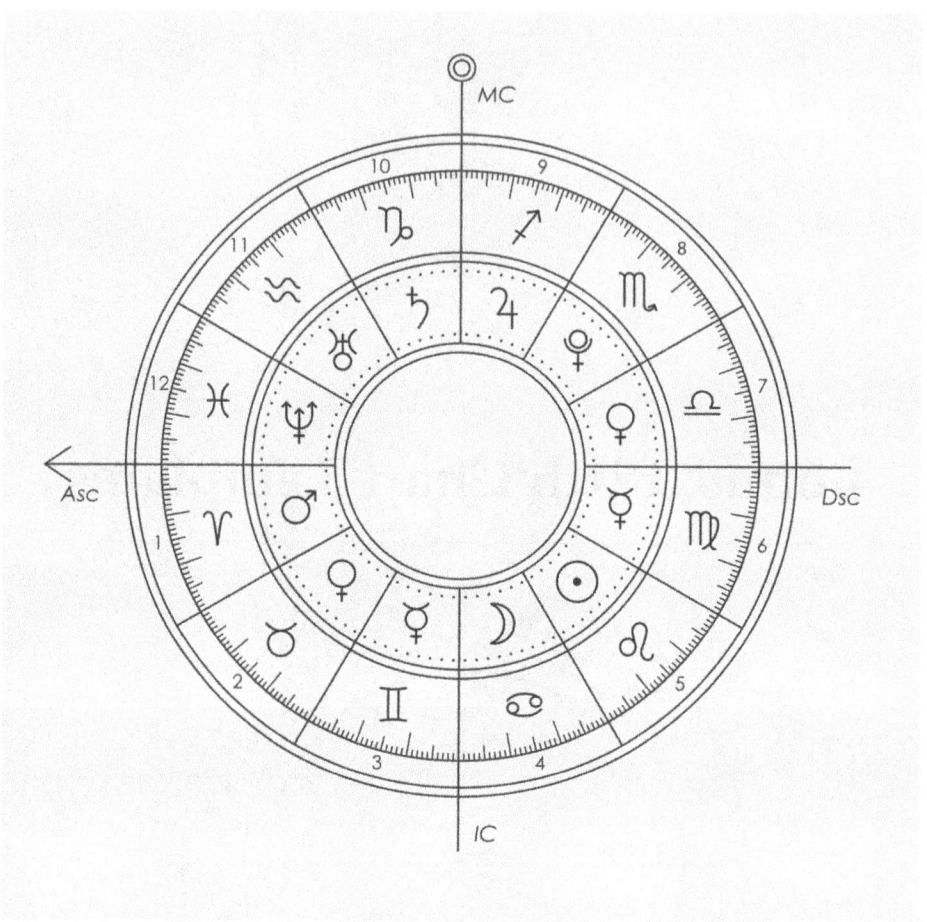

Birth chart template.

# Conclusion

As you're at the end of this book, it is time to reflect on what you have learned. Throughout the pages, you have explored the intricacies of birth charts and how they offer insight into your unique personality and life path. You have learned about the different components of birth charts, such as the sun sign, moon sign, and rising sign, and how they work together to create a complex and dynamic picture of who you are.

Beyond the technical side of birth charts, you have also delved into the deeper philosophical and spiritual aspects of astrology. You have learned about the interconnectedness of all things and the ways in which astrology can help you understand your place in the world. You have explored the idea of destiny and free will and how they intersect in your life.

Remember that astrology is not a one-size-fits-all solution. Your birth chart is unique to you, and no two charts are alike. Therefore, approach astrology with an open mind and a willingness to explore and experiment. Don't be afraid to trust your instincts and interpret your chart in a way that feels authentic to you.

As the famous astrologer Linda Goodman once said, "Your birth chart is a snapshot of the sky at the moment you were born. It reveals your potential and your purpose, and it can help guide you on your journey through life."

Another important lesson that astrology teaches is that we are all connected. You are a part of the same cosmic web as everyone else, and your life is intertwined with others in ways you may not even realize.

Therefore, it's important for you to approach life with empathy and compassion and to treat others as you would like to be treated.

One of the things you may appreciate most about astrology is its ability to offer guidance and support in times of uncertainty. When you're feeling lost or confused, your birth chart can act as a lighthouse, guiding you toward your true north. It can help you see the bigger picture and understand your place in the grand scheme of things.

But perhaps the most important lesson that astrology teaches is that you are unique and special in your own way. You have your own strengths and weaknesses, challenges, and opportunities. And it's up to you to make the most of what you've been given, to embrace your quirks and idiosyncrasies, and to live your life to the fullest.

If you enjoyed this book, I'd greatly appreciate a review on Amazon because it helps me to create more books that people want. It would mean a lot to hear from you.

**To leave a review:**

1. Open your camera app.
2. Point your mobile device at the QR code.
3. The review page will appear in your web browser.

---

*Thanks for your support!*

# Here's another book by Mari Silva that you might like

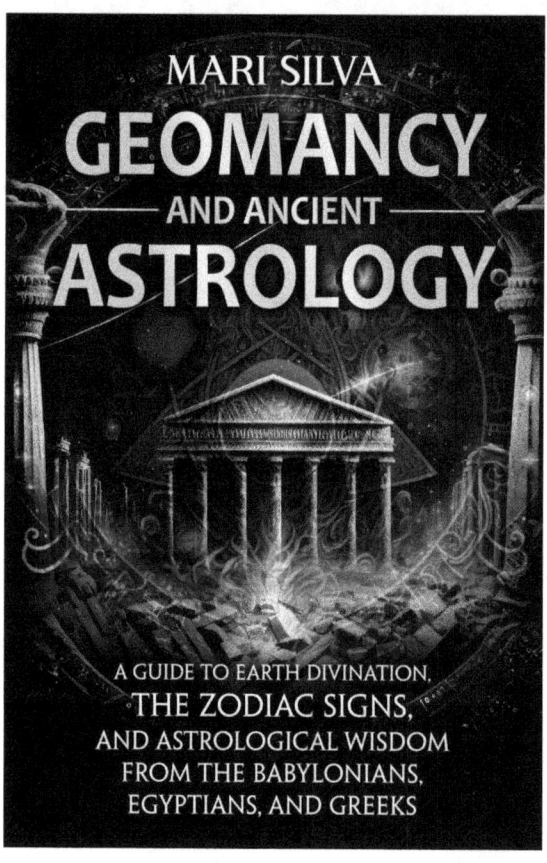

# Your Free Gift
# (only available for a limited time)

Thanks for getting this book! If you want to learn more about various spirituality topics, then join Mari Silva's community and get a free guided meditation MP3 for awakening your third eye. This guided meditation mp3 is designed to open and strengthen ones third eye so you can experience a higher state of consciousness. Simply visit the link below the image to get started.

https://spiritualityspot.com/meditation

Or, Scan the QR code!

# References

**Part 1: The Twelve Houses of Astrology**

Brown, M. (2022, December 12). The 12 houses of astrology, explained. InStyle. https://www.instyle.com/12-houses-of-astrology-6890300

Kelly, A. (2018, October 6). What Houses in your birth chart mean, and how to find them. Allure. https://www.allure.com/story/12-astrology-houses-meaning

Lanyadoo, J. (2019, August 19). Here's everything you need to know about astrology houses. Cosmopolitan. https://www.cosmopolitan.com/lifestyle/a28700440/astrology-houses/

Mazurek, D. (2022, November 16). What do the 12 houses mean in astrology? Dictionary.com. https://www.dictionary.com/e/what-do-the-houses-mean-in-astrology/

The Editors of Encyclopedia Britannica. (2022). zodiac. In Encyclopedia Britannica.

Tomar, D. (2019, May 30). Learn about the 12 houses in Vedic astrology. AstroTalk Blog - Online Astrology Consultation with Astrologer; AstroTalk. https://astrotalk.com/astrology-blog/houses-in-vedic-astrology/

Wright, J. (2022, January 2). What are the 12 houses of astrology? PureWow. https://www.purewow.com/wellness/12-houses-of-astrology

**Part 2: Birth Charts**

(N.d.-a). Cafeastrology.com. https://cafeastrology.com/birthchartinterpretations.html

(N.d.-a). Chaninicholas.com. https://chaninicholas.com/what-whole-sign-houses-are-and-why-we-use-them/

(N.d.-b). Astrology.com. https://www.astrology.com/article/sun-moon-rising-zodiac-signs.html

(N.d.-b). Visionimediterranee.It. https://nhlkgy.visionimediterranee.it/porphyry-birth-chart.html

(N.d.-c). Astrostyle.com. https://astrostyle.com/rising-sign-calculator/

(N.d.-d). Astrologyking.com. https://astrologyking.com/descendant/

(N.d.-e). Astrologylibrary.org. https://www.astrologylibrary.org/interpretations/midheaven/

10 Talents Revealed in Astrological Charts. (2020, February 13). Dummies. https://www.dummies.com/article/body-mind-spirit/religion-spirituality/astrology/10-talents-revealed-in-astrological-charts-268205/

12 Zodiac Signs – dates, meanings & compatibility. (n.d.). Emma. https://emma.ca/zodiac-signs

A beginner's guide to the 12 houses of the horoscope. (2020, August 31). Mindbodygreen. https://www.mindbodygreen.com/articles/the-12-houses-of-astrology

Astrological birth charts for celebrities and famous people. (n.d.). Astro-charts.com. https://astro-charts.com/persons/

Astrological Keywords of Planets in Astrology. (2022, June 1). Paula Lustemberg. https://paulalustemberg.com/en/astrological-keywords-planets/

Astroyogi. (2019, December 7). The 12 houses of astrology and their significance. Yahoo News. https://www.yahoo.com/news/12-houses-astrology-significance-140205298.html

Brown, M. (2021, January 22). The complete guide to zodiac signs and their meanings. Shape. https://www.shape.com/lifestyle/mind-and-body/zodiac-signs-meanings-dates

Brown, M. (2022, July 19). Your astrological birth chart, explained. POPSUGAR. https://www.popsugar.com/smart-living/astrology-birth-chart-48875828

Celebrity Astro Databank – Celebrity Horoscope. (n.d.). Astrosage.com. http://astrosage.com/celebrity-horoscope/

Davis, F. (2021, September 13). The four quadrants in astrology: Where your main focus in this lifetime lies. Cosmic Cuts. https://cosmiccuts.com/blogs/healing-stones-blog/quadrants-in-astrology

de Vesle – Astrotheme, B. J.-P. L. (n.d.). Planets distribution and hemispheres. Astrotheme.com. https://www.astrotheme.com/planets-distribution.php

Explore Astrological Birth Charts of Famous People by Aspect. (n.d.). Astro-Charts.Com. https://astro-charts.com/persons/aspect/

Findyourfate.com Astrology: Minor Aspects in Astrology. https://astrology.findyourfate.com/astrology-minoraspects.html

Garis, M. G. (2020, March 31). How to Read a Natal Chart—Planets, Symbols, and All. Well+Good. https://www.wellandgood.com/how-to-read-natal-chart/

Hemisphere emphasis. (2015, April 17). Cafeastrology.com; Cafe Astrology.com. https://cafeastrology.com/articles/hemisphereemphasis.html

Herbst, B. (1988). Houses of the horoscope. ACS Publications.

How to read your birth chart like an astrologer. (2019, January 31). Mindbodygreen. https://www.mindbodygreen.com/articles/how-to-read-your-astrology-birth-chart

Jarus, O. (2012, January 16). Good heavens! Oldest-known astrologer's board discovered. Live Science. https://www.livescience.com/17943-oldest-astrologer-board-zodiac.html

Kelly, A. (2018, February 2). 12 zodiac signs: Dates and personality traits of each star sign. Allure. https://www.allure.com/story/zodiac-sign-personality-traits-dates

Kelly, A. (2022, August 22). Astrology birth charts 101. The Cut. https://www.thecut.com/article/astrology-birth-chart-meaning-analysis.html

Kelly, A. (2022, November 24). A Handy Guide to Astrology's Black Moon Lilith. The Cut. https://www.thecut.com/2022/11/black-moon-lilith-astrology-meaning.html

Koch house system. (n.d.). Astro.com. https://www.astro.com/astrowiki/en/Koch_House_System

Lanyadoo, J. (2011, May 21). How to read an astrology chart. WikiHow. https://www.wikihow.com/Read-an-Astrology-Chart

Lieberman, R. (2020, December 18). The Magic of the North Node in Astrology and Human Design. Pure Generators. https://www.puregenerators.com/blog/north-nodes-in-astrology-and-human-design

Lundquist, P. (2022, January 19). Hemispheres in astrology: Life themes. The Happy Mystic. https://thehappymystic.com/hemispheres-astrology/

Magner, E. (2022, October 4). The 12 houses in astrology can help you understand a new level of your zodiac sign. Well+Good. https://www.wellandgood.com/houses-in-astrology/

Mahtani, N. (2020, March 31). Your astrology birth chart reveals more than you might expect. Nylon. https://www.nylon.com/astrology-birth-chart

Maria. (2021, July 9). Minor Aspects in Astrology: Helpful Guide to Astrology. Trusted Astrology. https://trusted-astrology.com/minor-aspects-in-astrology/

Munson, O. (2023, February 6). How many Zodiac signs are there? Meet the 12 astrological signs, their traits and more. USA Today.

https://www.usatoday.com/story/life/2023/02/06/how-many-zodiac-signs/11039695002/

Odyssey, D. (2021, October 29). Asteroids In Astrology & Their Meanings, Explained. Nylon. https://www.nylon.com/life/asteroids-astrology-meaning

Orion, R. (2020, February 13). How to identify overall patterns on your astrological birth chart. Dummies. https://www.dummies.com/article/body-mind-spirit/religion-spirituality/astrology/how-to-identify-overall-patterns-on-your-astrological-birth-chart-268214/

Placidus house system. (n.d.). Astro.com. https://www.astro.com/astrowiki/en/Placidus_House_System

Rao, J. (2008, May 30). How the ecliptic and the zodiac work. Space. https://www.space.com/5417-ecliptic-zodiac-work.html

Regan, S. (2022, April 19). The Most & Least Lucky Aspects To Have On Your Zodiac Chart, From Astrologers. Mindbodygreen. https://www.mindbodygreen.com/articles/aspects-in-astrology

Rob Tillett, I. T. (n.d.). Astrology on the Web: Nodes, Chiron & Asteroids, Ceres, Pallas Athene, Juno & Vesta. Astrologycom.Com. https://www.astrologycom.com/aster.html

Rose, K. (2020, May 20). A Guide To The Minor Aspects In Astrology — And What They Mean For Your Life. YourTango. https://www.yourtango.com/2020333329/what-are-minor-aspects-astrology-what-they-mean-for-your-life-horoscope

stargazer. (2021, August 13). Minor Aspects in Astrology: Quincunx, Semisquare, Semi-Sextile, Quintile. Astrology. https://advanced-astrology.com/minor-aspects/

Temporal Houses. (n.d.). Astrologyweekly.com. https://www.astrologyweekly.com/dictionary/temporal-houses.php

The AstroTwins. (2020, August 15). The 4 Essential Dignities of Planets: Exalted, Detriment, Domicile and Fall. Astrostyle: Astrology and Daily, Weekly, Monthly Horoscopes by The AstroTwins. https://astrostyle.com/astrology/essential-dignities/

The Editors of Encyclopedia Britannica. (2023). zodiac. In Encyclopedia Britannica.

The Meaning of the Aspects in Astrology. (2015, April 15). Cafeastrology.Com. https://cafeastrology.com/articles/aspectsinastrology.html

The most & least lucky aspects to have on your zodiac chart, from astrologers. (2022, April 19). Mindbodygreen. https://www.mindbodygreen.com/articles/aspects-in-astrology

Thomas, K. (2021, November 16). What is a birth chart in astrology — and how do you read one? New York Post. https://nypost.com/article/astrology-birth-chart/

Thomas, K. (2022, March 15). Your Guide to Planetary Aspects. Cosmopolitan. https://www.cosmopolitan.com/lifestyle/a37341996/astrology-aspects-list/

Thomas, K. (2022, March 15). Your Guide to Planetary Aspects. Cosmopolitan. https://www.cosmopolitan.com/lifestyle/a37341996/astrology-aspects-list/

Williams, M. (2022a, February 2). I don't know my birth time. How can I work with my birth chart & astrology? Chani Nicholas. https://chaninicholas.com/how-can-i-work-with-my-astrology-chart-if-i-dont-know-my-birth-time/

Williams, M. (2022b, March 31). What is a birth chart in astrology? Chani Nicholas. https://chaninicholas.com/what-is-a-birth-chart/

# Image Sources

1 Wellcome Library, London, CC BY 4.0 <https://creativecommons.org/licenses/by/4.0>, via Wikimedia Commons https://commons.wikimedia.org/wiki/File:Astrologer_of_the_Brahmin_caste,_India,_c_1825_Wellcome_L0035997.jpg

2 CactiStaccingCrane, CC BY-SA 4.0 <https://creativecommons.org/licenses/by-sa/4.0>, via Wikimedia Commons https://commons.wikimedia.org/wiki/File:Solar_System_true_color.jpg

3 https://freesvg.org/sun-and-fish-ancient-symbol

4 https://freesvg.org/illustration-of-a-symbol-with-crescent-shape-and-a-circle

5 https://www.needpix.com/photo/download/30682/planet-symbols-mercury-astronomical-planetary-astrological-astrology-free-vector-graphics-free-pictures

6 Font Awesome Free 5.2.0 by @fontawesome - https://fontawesome.com, CC BY 4.0 <https://creativecommons.org/licenses/by/4.0>, via Wikimedia Commons https://upload.wikimedia.org/wikipedia/commons/6/66/Font_Awesome_5_solid_venus-mars.svg

7 Kwamikagami, CC BY-SA 4.0 <https://creativecommons.org/licenses/by-sa/4.0>, via Wikimedia Commons https://commons.wikimedia.org/wiki/File:Mars_symbol.svg

8 Creative Commons CC0 1.0 Universal Public Domain Dedication < https://creativecommons.org/publicdomain/zero/1.0/deed.en> https://upload.wikimedia.org/wikipedia/commons/5/5a/Rma_-_lh.svg

9 Firkin CC0 1.0 Universal (CC0 1.0) Public Domain Dedication https://creativecommons.org/publicdomain/zero/1.0/ https://openclipart.org/detail/227759/solar-system-symbols

10 Firkin CC0 1.0 Universal (CC0 1.0) Public Domain Dedication

https://creativecommons.org/publicdomain/zero/1.0/ Solar system symbols - Openclipart

11 State Farm, CC BY 2.0 <https://creativecommons.org/licenses/by/2.0>, via Wikimedia Commons https://commons.wikimedia.org/wiki/File:Asteroid_falling_to_Earth.jpg

12 DG-RA CC0 1.0 Universal (CC0 1.0) Public Domain Dedication, https://creativecommons.org/publicdomain/zero/1.0/
https://openclipart.org/detail/307964/signs-of-the-zodiacs

13 https://pixabay.com/es/photos/reloj-astronomico-praga-226897/

14 This file is licensed under the Creative Commons Attribution-Share Alike 4.0 International license. <https://creativecommons.org/licenses/by-sa/4.0/deed.en> https://upload.wikimedia.org/wikipedia/commons/c/c7/Whole_Sign_house_divisions.jpg

15 Rursus, CC BY-SA 3.0 <https://creativecommons.org/licenses/by-sa/3.0>, via Wikimedia Commons: https://commons.wikimedia.org/wiki/File:Birth_chart.svg

16 EN NOIR & BLANC, CC0, via Wikimedia Commons: https://commons.wikimedia.org/wiki/File:Zodiaque._Zodiac._Book_illustration_(encyclopedia_plate,_line_art)_Larousse_du_XX%C3%A8me_si%C3%A8cle_1932.png

17 Macalves, CC BY-SA 4.0 <https://creativecommons.org/licenses/by-sa/4.0>, via Wikimedia Commons: https://commons.wikimedia.org/wiki/File:Whole_Sign_house_divisions.jpg

18 Macalves, CC BY-SA 4.0 <https://creativecommons.org/licenses/by-sa/4.0>, via Wikimedia Commons: https://commons.wikimedia.org/wiki/File:Porphyry_house_divisions.jpg

19 Macalves, CC BY-SA 4.0 <https://creativecommons.org/licenses/by-sa/4.0>, via Wikimedia Commons: https://commons.wikimedia.org/wiki/File:Koch_house_divisions.jpg

20 Image by Gordon Johnson from Pixabay https://pixabay.com/images/id-5921179/

21 Eaterjolly, CC BY-SA 4.0 <https://creativecommons.org/licenses/by-sa/4.0>, via Wikimedia Commons: https://commons.wikimedia.org/wiki/File:TP_mun_EN_moon.svg

22 MarcusWerthmann, CC BY-SA 3.0 <https://creativecommons.org/licenses/by-sa/3.0>, via Wikimedia Commons https://commons.wikimedia.org/wiki/File:Gender-Symbol_Hermaphrodite_Mercury_dark_transparent_Background.png

23 https://commons.wikimedia.org/wiki/File:Psi2.svg

24 Morn, CC BY-SA 3.0 <https://creativecommons.org/licenses/by-sa/3.0>, via Wikimedia Commons: https://commons.wikimedia.org/wiki/File:Natal_Chart_--_Adam.svg

www.ingramcontent.com/pod-product-compliance
Lightning Source LLC
Chambersburg PA
CBHW051854160426
43209CB00006B/1295